CLINT BLACK:
A Better Man

by R. D. Brown

A Fireside Book
Published by Simon & Schuster
New York London Toronto Sydney Tokyo Singapore

F FIRESIDE
Simon & Schuster Building
Rockefeller Center
1230 Avenue of the Americas
New York, New York 10020

Copyright © 1993 by R. D. Brown and RHK/Creative Services
Produced by RHK/Creative Services
Designed by Michaelis/Carpelis Design Assoc. Inc.

Manufactured in the United States of America.

1 3 5 7 9 10 8 6 4 2

Library of Congress Cataloging-in-Publication Data
is available.

ISBN 0-671-86546-3

CONTENTS

Photo Credits for Color Insert

ACKNOWLEDGMENTS

I would like to thank the following people for all their help and support:

Above all, I would like to thank Rhonda Markowitz, without whom this book might not have been written.

I would also like to thank Michael Shore; not only has he made me laugh on a consistent basis, he has also helped me become a much better writer and reporter. Thanks, too, to the dynamic duo, Sue Flinker and Dara. My gratitude to Risa Kessler, with hopes that her faith has not gone unrewarded.

On the business side, I am grateful to the people who were so generous with their time and energy: Rick Mitchell at the *Houston Chronicle*, Ed Morris at *Billboard's* Nashville outpost, Alanna Nash at large (currently toiling in the court of the King, taking notes with the members of the Memphis Mafia), Claudia Perry at the *Houston Post*, Chris Bell and Alex Reppen at Machattan, Marie Ratliff at *Amusement Business*, Steve Simels at *Entertainment Weekly*, and Ronnie Pugh at the Country Music Foundation.

On the personal end, I must thank my long-suffering friends, who offered support, encouragement, and understanding when I couldn't come out and play. They include (but are not limited to) Wendy Blatt, Carolyn Churchill, Kathy Davis, and all the fine folks at MTV News, Maria Del Greco, Jim Farber, Marianne Goldstein, Eric Gregg, Rick Hamilton, Bibbe Hansen, Dan Hedges, Auchee Lee, Virginia Lohle, Laurie Paladino, Ebet Roberts, Andrew Scrivener, Lori Somes, Lisa Zimmerman and Steve Weitzman. (If I have inadvertently slighted anyone, mea culpa: put it down to deadline amnesia.)

Thanks are due to the writers and reporters whose work has been used in the writing of this book. I wish I could thank them all personally; their contributions, however unwitting, have been invaluable. And thanks to all the photographers, who receive little respect for a grueling job. Someday their work will be appreciated for the art form that it truly is.

This book is dedicated to Kate and Isadore Markowitz, and to Roz Black (no relation to Clint). They have been my best friends since day one, and I can never repay them. Consider this a small deposit on my account.

                    Ron D. Brown
                    November 1992

CLINT BLACK:

A Better Man

INTRODUCTION

The essential Clint Black, serious and soulful, in performance at the Universal Amphitheater in Los Angeles, April 1992.

On July 16, 1989, Clint headlined a benefit concert in Staten Island, New York, to help raise funds for a local family's medical expenses.

Clint Black is one lucky cowboy, and don't think he doesn't know it.

In just a few years, the thirty-year-old singer-song-writer has gone from playing for peanuts on the cock-tail circuit around Houston to audiences averaging ten thousand people a night. His current concert tour— which began in July 1992 and will take him to 150 cities before it ends in March 1993—is expected to draw 1.5 million paying customers, who will watch Black perform on a stage costing $250,000. In 1991, Black was number nine on *Amusement Business* magazine's list of the top ten tours, grossing $12.6 million in ticket sales.

In 1989, Black's first album, *Killin' Time*, was released. He was named Most Promising Newcomer by the Country Music Association; the album garnered three Grammy Award nomina-tions and yielded five number one country singles — a record for a debut album, which remains unbroken. To date, with just three albums to his name, Black has sold over five million records. This enables the former high school dropout to afford a 180-acre ranch outside Houston and a home by the lake in Nashville. Then there's the four-bedroom dwelling in the Hollywood hills that Black shares

4

with his bride, the feline television actress Lisa Hartman. And as if all this weren't enough, his recent marriage makes him wax positively rhapsodic. "I look at her and think, boy, did I get lucky!"

THE COUNTRY MUSIC BOOM

How did Clint Black get so darn lucky, anyway?

Not to take anything away from the man and his talent—but timing is everything, as they say, and Black's timing is exquisite. He happened to break upon the country music scene just as the popularity of the genre went through the roof—and Black went right along with it, becoming the best-selling country artist on his record label (RCA) while he was at it.

Anyone with even a passing interest in popular culture could not have failed to notice the recent boom in all things country-western. Country music is no longer the province of poor rural folks, complete with a sad-eyed beagle out by the moonshine still. Rather, it has spread its net wide, reaching everyone from the youngest children to the most senior citizens in all parts of the country. This remarkable feat has been accomplished rapidly; according to the Recording Industry Association of America (RIAA), sales of country music grew to 12.5 percent of total music sales in 1991, up from 8.8 percent the previous year. In 1988 and 1989, country music held only a 6.8 percent share. While country still trails rock (which commands 36.3 percent of the $7.8 billion U.S. market), other statistics verify the surge. In 1991, country acts increased their concert ticket sales by 40 percent, as income for the top ten pop and rock acts declined 32 percent. Country fans purchase more than $700 million worth of recorded music annually; in 1991, thirty-five country albums went platinum, signifying sales of at least one million copies each. This is in stark contrast to 1985, when only sixteen country albums went gold, meaning they only sold over five hundred thousand copies apiece.

The number of country music radio stations in America has grown from 1,500 in 1980 to over 2,600 today. In nearly half of the biggest U.S. markets, a country station ranks number one. TNN, the Nashville-based country cable television network, grew from seven million subscribers in 1985 to fifty-three million in 1991. Country music fan clubs have been established in places as far away as England, Japan, and Australia. And in Branson, Missouri, a tiny dot (population: 3,706) deep in the Ozark

5

Mountains, more than two dozen theaters devoted to country music draw more than four million people annually, who drop $750 million while they're in town. Fan Fair, the Nashville celebration where fans and stars meet and greet every June, has been sold out months in advance for the past two years as twenty-four thousand attendees cheerfully pay the $75 admission fee.

While golden-agers are learning the two-step down at the local YMCA, Walt Disney Records is putting out a *Country Music for Kids* album, featuring artists as diverse as the legendary Merle Haggard, Grammy-Award winner Mary-Chapin Carpenter, country-rock avatar Emmylou Harris, and Glen "Wichita Lineman"

6

Campbell. Campbell, a father of eight, says, "Country music is a lot more family-oriented. ...This is a good little idea."

Country music is one of the few growth industries in a recessionary America, and there's no end in sight. The new country boom has been a healthy shot in the arm for breweries, who tie in promotional support with country tours (Clint Black is sponsored by Miller Brewing). Clothing manufacturers and retailers, too, have found country's new popularity a solid-gold bonanza; the makers of cowboy hats, boots, belt buckles, bolo ties, and fancy shirts, and the blue jean industry all have reason to celebrate. Then there's the auxiliary market—such as the new magazines devoted to country music stars—and the merchandising of everything from posters to key rings, all being snapped up at an astonishing rate. Those who were caught unprepared were left wondering how to catch up and what in the blue blazes was going on.

THE EVOLUTION OF COUNTRY MUSIC

For one thing, country has changed. It used to be cornball, with the television series *Hee-Haw* a prime example: outhouse humor, Daisy-Mae, the farmer's daughters, Grand Ole Opry veterans such as Minnie Pearl. It was associated with vulgarity and tacky glitter; remember the gold lamé suit once worn by Elvis, the original Hillbilly Cat? It was only one of a long line of elaborate outfits created by Nudie, tailor to the earliest country stars (including the sainted Hank Williams, Senior). Country used to be decidedly uncool; as one twenty-six-year-old man said recently, "In the seventies...you never, never admitted to listening to western [music]. Now they're getting to the point where it's considered hip."

An influx of younger stars like Black, Travis Tritt, Alan Jackson, and Ricky Van Shelton has helped. So have singers who have forcibly dragged the music over boundaries it never thought to cross before: the gender-bending of k.d. lang, the feminist sensibilities of K. T. Oslin and Mary-Chapin Carpenter, the pop crossover of Billy Ray Cyrus. And, of course, there's the unprecedented success of Garth Brooks, a man who modestly describes his own face as resembling "a thumb with a hat on it." Be that as it may, Brooks is the one who broke down all the barriers, big time, and a new way to monitor record sales proved it.

Billboard magazine is the final word in the music industry. Its charts that track record sales and radio airplay are considered the world standard. But for years the magazine relied on a rather archaic method of accounting, allowing record store managers and radio program directors to report their biggest sellers (or requests) verbally, with no supporting evidence. It doesn't take an Einstein to figure out how an enterprising record promotion man (the field is almost exclusively male) could apply coercion or a little friendly gift in order to obtain the numbers he was hired to produce. When *Billboard* adopted the SoundScan system in 1991, all that went out the window.

SoundScan operates in much the same way as a computerized supermarket register; it reads the bar code on a cassette or compact disc upon purchase, just like frozen peas at the local A&P. For a few weeks after *Billboard* went online with SoundScan, the charts looked like a crazy quilt. Records were coming in at number one—once a rare feat—and then dropping rapidly, while other albums bounced all over the place. There was one artist, though, whose third record came in at number one on the pop charts, where it stayed like a phonograph needle stuck in the groove. Then, after his first two records lodged firmly at positions five and ten and lingered for months on end, everyone had to take notice of Garth Brooks. Much like "the man who came to dinner," he would not go away.

Although country seems to have had a startling impact very quickly, it didn't happen overnight. Marketing executives and critics who cover popular music have attempted to pinpoint exactly when this new country boom began. Discounting the mechanical-bull fad that surfaced briefly after the release of the film *Urban Cowboy*, many professionals feel the first major country ground swell began in 1986, when Randy Travis released his debut record. Ed Miller, *Billboard*'s country editor, says, "I don't know anyone who's had the impact of Randy Travis." Just twenty-two at the time, Travis was a young, good-looking alternative to the older generation of performers that included such stalwarts as Johnny Cash and George Jones. While Travis was—and is—a fine singer and songwriter, his success was due at least in part to his appeal to women, who are believed to be the primary listeners to country music.

College students were also getting into country, defying the traditional wisdom that said they were only attracted to the more "alternative" types of music. Their older siblings, now in their thirties and forties, were jumping genres, too. Once they had listened almost exclusively to rock; now they were primed for the emergence of this new kind of country music, because they had been hearing variations on this theme for years.

Rock and roll has always included country-oriented music under its generous umbrella. The Beatles covered Carl Perkins ("Matchbox," "Honey Don't") early in their career. The Byrds, the Flying Burrito Brothers, the Band, James Taylor, the Eagles, and Bob Dylan (especially during his "Nashville Skyline" period) demonstrated country influences. Even the Rolling Stones, who had first dabbled in country back in 1964 when they covered Hank Snow's "I'm Movin' On," gave it another shot five years later

Following his Carnegie Hall performance in 1989, Clint received a plaque commemorating the #1 status of his debut album, Killin' Time.

with "Honky Tonk Women" and "Country Honk" on their 1969 *Let It Bleed* LP, influenced by guitarist Keith Richards' friendship with Burrito founder Gram Parsons. John Mellencamp made some of his most heartfelt (and successful) music after he shed his "Cougar" rock persona and returned to his heartland roots in 1985 with the critically acclaimed *Scarecrow* album. So it's not hard to understand why country's new audience included baby-boomer rock fans: they were already accustomed to the sound and feel of the music.

And yet, there's more to the new country than familiarity. Those rock fans, now hitting middle age, are confronting things they never thought would happen to them: receding hairlines, cellulite, and a sorrowful sense of diminished possibilities. Country, more than any other musical genre, speaks to these eternal verities. Scott Miller, a corporate and political strategist, told the *Boston Globe*, "There's both an economic and psychological deceleration out of the eighties, something like the astronauts used to experience coming into the atmosphere. There's an awful lot of people rejecting yuppiness, and all the psychologists are seeing a return to basic values."

Besides all the highfalutin psychospeak, there are the ears and minds of battered consumers to consider. The simple fact is that sometimes other types of contemporary music can be too harsh. A twenty-six-year-old from Fargo, North Dakota, told the *Minneapolis Star-Tribune*, "When I was in high school, I used to listen to Def Leppard and heavy metal. Country was weird. Now country is cool. As you get older, songs tell a story and you can appreciate that." Others can't take the sound of urban music, like rap. One country executive boasted, "Every time they play a rap record, they send thousands over to our side."

As if in confirmation, more than twelve-hundred nightclubs specializing in country music have sprung up like so many wildflowers across America, serving a diverse clientele in some pretty unlikely locales. In New York City, which—firepower aside—is hardly an outpost of the wild West, a number of country-flavored clubs with names like the Rodeo Bar and the Cheatin' Heart Cafe have appeared. In Santa Monica, California, Denim and Diamonds is doing a brisk business in country—less than a year ago, the club played Top 40 hits. Many people find the laid-back atmosphere of the newer country-western clubs comfortable, lacking the pretension and overt sexuality usually associated with bars; and this feeling is not limited to heterosexuals.

In a development that caught many in Nashville by surprise, country-themed nights in gay clubs have taken off. The manager of a club called Saddle Up, located in president-elect Bill Clinton's headquarters of Little Rock, Arkansas, told *Billboard*, "I think the big misconception about gay men and their musical tastes is that we all love disco or the opera. The fact is, a lot of the men who come here relate very closely to the music. They bond with the fact that [country is] openly emotional and yet extremely masculine." But the hunk quotient of today's crop of young male country stars certainly doesn't hurt. As one patron of the Chute in Nashville puts it, "We simply want to lust after them from a distance and enjoy their music." If truth be told, that desire is not so different from that felt by many female fans.

Especially when it comes to Clint Black. He's the type of man who doesn't threaten other men, but he sure drives the ladies wild. As Buck Owens put it, "He's the kind of guy you'd want to take home to meet your father, if you could trust your mother." Female fans regularly attempt to get closer to him while he's onstage. Black still remembers one Canadian lady who hit him "at about twenty miles an hour." One twenty-three-year old female fan in attendance at a 1992 Houston Astrodome concert was thrilled just to be in Black's general vicinity. "I love his music, and, boy, is he cute," she gushed. "He's got the sweetest smile." A review of a Seattle Center Coliseum concert in September 1991 elaborated. "His blue eyes sparkled so brightly under his cowboy hat you could see them from twenty rows back. Female fans pelted the stage with flowers throughout the ninety-minute set, when they weren't jumping up and down and screaming."

The sweet smile and pretty eyes are fortunate genetic gifts, and Black is grateful for the attention, but not at the expense of his credibility. "I've always believed in my music," he says firmly. "I think that's first and foremost." He takes the sex-symbol stuff with a grain of salt because "I still maintain that nothing matters but the music, and that's why I'm here." He's determined to be taken seriously, even if it is an uphill battle. And, as we will see, he is accustomed to winning. . . even if it is "the hard way."

Ladies and gentlemen . . . Clint Black.

IN
THE
BEGINNING

Future country singing sensation Clint Black made his worldly debut on February 4, 1962, in Long Branch, New Jersey. That's where his father, G. A., was temporarily working on a pipeline. "I wasn't there but six months," Clint said, before G. A. and Ann decided to take a chance and move the family (Clint and his three older brothers: Mark, born in 1957, Brian, in '58 and Kevin, '59) to Spring Branch, Texas, a suburb of Houston. By the time he was in high school, the Blacks had moved to Katy, about fifteen miles west of Houston. Black's success has made both towns proudly claim him as their own.

Black characterized his adolescence as typical, in a blue-collar rural-suburban sort of way. His days were filled with activities any all-American boy might explore in such a bucolic setting: hunting snakes, camping, fishing,and building tree houses and forts in the woods. He took his skateboard almost everywhere. He seemed happy and well adjusted, except for the fact that he was sensitive about a physical characteristic he was powerless to change: his height.

13

Clint was four feet nine inches until he was in the tenth grade, while his older brothers were big and muscular. Those who know him best speculate that growing up "shrimpy" in a state like Texas, where bigger is always better, drove the youngster to seek recognition any way he could. His brother Brian thinks the fact that Clint was so much smaller than his siblings had a lot to do with his drive to succeed. "Clint has always been so determined," Brian

A return trip to Sherlock's Pub in Houston, this time with the host and crew from TNT's "Crook and Chase" television show, 1990.

said. "He never quit. In high school, he was painfully short. I think it's one of the things that brought him to have the willpower he does." Black, who eventually grew to a respectable five feet nine inches, would take that willpower and apply it to his one passion with single minded devotion.

GROWING UP MUSICAL

Black admits to having been obsessed with music as far back as he can recall. Even as a small child, he was listening to the blues, soaking up the keening vocals and gutbucket guitar, drawn to the pain and redemption he heard there. "When I was eight years old, I was imitating the blues masters. I love the blues; that's where everything came from, as far as pop music goes. I was listening to that at a real early age." Two years later, he had begun making his first attempts to woo an audience. "I'd go from table to table at Bear Creek Park, singing to anybody who'd listen."

At thirteen, he swiped a harmonica from one of his brothers, becoming a familiar sight as he careened through the neighborhood on his skateboard, playing the harp and practicing his breath control. At fifteen, "I taught myself guitar, taught myself

14

how to sing, and started writing songs as soon as I learned some chords. . . . I learned everything by ear." Black confessed, "I couldn't tell you what notes make up a chord, I just play 'em . . . . When I learned three or four songs, I ran around the neighborhood and would play 'em over and over for anyone and everyone. All my friends said, 'You've got a great voice, you're gonna be a star someday.' In Houston, if you sounded halfway decent, they thought you'd end up on the radio someday. They told me, and I believed them. I was probably sixteen, and I decided, this is what I was gonna do."

Ann Black recalled, "Clint just loved an audience. Sometimes he'd get out his guitar with the kids on the back porch and sing for them. Or he and Kevin would sit in the kitchen and play while I was fixing supper." His dad remembered, "When he was about fourteen, I guess that's when I first noticed he had a great voice. He started playing the harmonica, and then he started singing along with the songs on the radio. He could copy most of 'em pretty good," said G. A. (The initials don't stand for anything —that's his name.) "He wrote his first song when he was fifteen, but I don't think he'll ever record it. It's not country. He liked everything so

Hayden Nicholas (second from left) and Clint after winning an ASCAP songwriting award. With them are Richard Perna, Howlin' Hits Music (far left) and John Briggs, ASCAP.

much, he just really didn't know what he wanted to do. He does great blues. I think he could sing opera if he wanted to."

Black remembered those days vividly. "People told me ever since I was a teenager that I was going to become a star. I wanted it so bad. . . . In high school, I was a loner." He admitted, "I wasn't popular with girls until I sang in the talent show in my junior year. I won second place, and I got all this attention." It was surprisingly easy, he found, to develop a taste for applause.

Ironically, it was the eldest son, Mark, who received the first guitar lessons when he was twelve. When the older Black brothers formed a band, Clint took up the bass to join them. "One minute we're playing 'Redneck Mother,'" he recalled, "and the next minute we're doing 'Long Distance Runaround' by Yes." Musical inclinations may have a genetic basis in the Black family: Clint claimed his Sicilian great-grandfather played violin with an orchestra that once toured America.   Instead of being driven crazy by four noisy young uns, G. A. and Ann were remarkably tolerant of their offspring's forays into music making. They encouraged the kids to play, luring neighbors and friends over to the house with barbecues in the backyard. There were times they got going so good, Black told *TIME* magazine in 1990, that the police would show up to reprimand them. "Folks next door, they're complaining," one cop dryly told the family on one such occasion. "Must not have invited them."

Today, both Brian and Kevin Black have attempted to make

Brian Black, who used to have trouble remembering more than a few songs at a time, focuses on a grassroots, traditional country sound.

17

their own mark on the country music world, with limited success, even though the *Houston Press* found that "Kevin's voice is raspier, naughtier than Clint's; Brian's is cleaner, even better." Kevin was the brother whose Full House Band Clint played in for five years; they later went on to perform as a duo during the happy hour in the Houston club scene. But it wasn't the happiest of times for the siblings. "Clint said I always turned it into the Kevin Black show, and nobody was listening to what he was singing," Kevin said ruefully. "He's a messenger, and he doesn't like anybody interfering with his message." Clint's older brother talks wistfully about working up an album, even though he doesn't perform any original material in his act. That hasn't discouraged the former ironworker, who is managed by Lou Bohan (the man who managed Clint for over six years, before his fateful meeting with Bill Ham.) Although Kevin has wishfully told the local press, "I need hundreds of thousands of people to play for," at one gig in late 1990, only fifty people showed up.

Brian Black, on the other hand, freely admitted, "I was never interested in struggling as hard as Kevin and Clint." Once a Harris County constable, Brian has the unfortunate reputation in the Black household as the one who can't remember more than a few songs at any one time, which didn't stop him from opening for Garth Brooks at county fairs several years back. Still, Brian said, "What I really wanted to be was a movie star." At the moment, though, only one of the Black boys is able to command the spotlight.

EARLY INFLUENCES

The moment of musical truth for him, as Black recalled it, was the day he first heard Merle Haggard's "Okie from Muskogee." "Man, I loved that song," Black enthused. "I liked the sound. I liked the lyrics—hell, back then it was the best thing we'd heard as far as music goes. I remember my mama callin' this DJ up in Houston one night to get him to play that song for me and my brothers. There we were, all gathered around the radio, and we hear this big voice sayin' "A-l-l-l right now, I'm a-gonna play that 'Okie from Muskogee' for them Black boys out there, who done told their mama that they ain't goin' to bed till they hear this song. Here it is, so you boys git!" Black laughed. "I tell you, that really had an effect on me. I took my music *real* serious after that."

G. A., said Clint, "was always bringing records home. He'd stop off on the way home from work and get a 45 and say, 'Listen to this, you oughta sing this song.'. . . I was exposed to everything, from what my dad had, like Webb Pierce, to Uriah Heep, Black Sabbath." The idea of a career in music, as farfetched as it appeared on the surface, began to seem like a real possibility to Clint. He knew he wasn't cut out for more academic pursuits after he dropped out of high school at seventeen. Up until he made the fateful decision, he'd spent most of his time in class writing poems and struggling with authority figures. He confessed that he "had a bad attitude. . . . I was like a lawyer at school. If I was in science class and we were doing laboratory tests, I would say, 'This can't be.' 'Well, it's an observation.' 'Wait a minute—*we* didn't see it!' I would challenge anything if I believed in it, and usually it was stupid stuff that got me nowhere.

"That's where my greatest regrets lie," Black went on. "I wish I'da gone to college and become a historian. *An* historian. I'd almost trade the success I have for the education I'd like to have." He briefly considered enlisting in the Air Force, thinking that he might one day train for NASA's space program. As it turned out, of course, the government's loss would become country music's gain, but not before some serious dues were paid.

Black soon had reason to regret his lack of a diploma. As bright and capable as he was, there weren't very many fast track occupations open to a dropout. While still a teenager, he took a "distribution" job with the *Houston Post*, selling newspaper subscriptions door-to-door. He remembered using his charm to great

Clint escorts his mother, Ann Black, to the Academy of Country Music Awards, April 1990. He won three awards that night, including Album of the Year (for Killin' Time).

19

effect: "I would knock on people's doors, have them slammed in my face, knock again, and try some way to ingratiate myself and talk about the paper. 'I noticed you have a boat in the garage. You must love boating. Man, they've got the greatest fishing column in there. . . .'" He did so well that his supervisors wanted to move him up to head a team, but in order to take advantage of the offer, he needed his own vehicle—which he did not have. He went on to labor as a bait cutter, fishing guide, and ironworker.

"I nearly fell off the seventh floor more than once," Black said of his construction work. "Once a load of concrete fell on me and completely covered me up. I've never been so angry in my life." He went on, "That's the job that did it. Man, that was the hardest thing that I have ever done; I have never been so miserable. One day I walked in and said, 'What in the hell am I doin'? Boys, I can sing—see you later,' and left. That was it." At this point, country music beckoned more seductively than ever. It wasn't just the lure of fortune and fame; Black longed to recapture the feeling he remembered from those backyard barbecues and talent shows. He decided that he had nothing to lose by making a grab for the brass ring.

Black began singing in the nightclubs around Houston, pasting up flyers to announce performances. "I don't think I saw a ten percent return on them," he said wryly. His first solo gig in Houston, in 1981, was followed by six years on the city's club circuit, playing everything from his beloved old blues to James Taylor covers. If a fan were to go on a pilgrimage to that city, retracing Black's steps to stardom, the places to check out would include Sherlock's Baker Street Pub, the Long Branch Café, Timothy's Pub, Lovejoy's (now Kelso's Rendezvous) and the Wunsche Brothers in Old Town Spring. Those who saw him at the time recall a "sensitive singer-songwriter Dan Fogelberg–type" up on the stage. Black wasn't too encouraged to keep going, he said, by the audiences he drew during his early days on the circuit. "I got some pats on the back at the break, but people wouldn't applaud and that's the main reason I'm doin' all this, for the response that I get from the people."

Audiences tend to resist original material, preferring to hear cover versions of songs they're already familiar with. Unfortunately, this attitude runs counter to the instincts of most performers who write songs of their own and want to get audi-

ence reaction to that original material. Black tried to hit a good balance, playing tunes penned by some of his own personal favorites. He is quick to cite James Taylor as one of his earliest influences ("I know a lot of his songs"), and adds a laundry list of other performers who have made a deep impression on him: "Merle Haggard. . . . Don Henley and Glenn Frey, Loggins & Messina, Jackson Browne . . . George Jones, Waylon Jennings, Jimmy Buffett. . . . Bob Seger, Steely Dan and Little Feat . . . Johnny Winter (and) Stevie Ray Vaughan."

In fact, Black was such a fan of Henley that he jumped at the chance to review the ex-Eagle's solo album, *The End of the Innocence*, for *PLAYBOY* magazine in October 1989. "Henley's

Kevin Black, an extremely versatile musician who describes his performing style as "aggressive country", looks foward to releasing an album one day.

21

affected me a lot," Black wrote. "He's written songs that helped shape my life, warned me about certain pitfalls, and, honestly, helped me *avoid* them. This is a great record—even if you just got the music without the lyrics, you'd be getting your money's worth. The title track hit me *so* hard—and you know if the first song on an album hits, you open yourself up to the rest. That lyrical hook line—you can *feel* the emotional weight of it.

"Elsewhere," Black continued, "like in 'Little Tin God,' some serious points about the world at large are made. The love songs come from the heart, but they have points to make, too. They made me look back at my love affairs. Henley must have been pulling from things he's been through. Almost *all* of his writing has real points to make. *The End of the Innocence* is the type of LP you'll listen to five years from now and get something you never caught before. The guy continues to inspire me."

His appreciation for the subtleties of a well-crafted song goes way back. Black recalled how he set himself apart from the other local musicians on the club circuit back in Houston. "I didn't play the current Top 40. You could go into any club and hear the same songs by every band, and even soloists would all have the same repertoire. I was reaching back and playing old stuff and obscure stuff from the hitmakers, songs off the album that you *didn't* hear." It was to Black's advantage that he possessed wide-ranging musical tastes, as he needed a varied set list to keep up his grueling schedule. "I'd play a happy-hour gig from five to seven for one hundred bucks, then work nine to one in another conversation bar for $150—six hours of singing a night! But I got by. . . . I think about it all the time." He says now, somewhat wistfully, "There's always something that takes me back to that."

From the start, Black said, he wanted to write his own material. He found himself "trying to observe everything I could about things that I knew would [someday] be a part of my past . . . things that I could never go back to. I figured that my life style would change if my dreams came true, so I needed to pay attention and remember what it's like to be standing on the side of the road with a flat tire and not have a spare—all those things that living on a bus or airplane you're not exposed to as much." He went on to reveal one of his songwriting secrets: "I used to go out and sit and watch people and have my napkins full of notes and little lines, just things that I would observe."

HAYDEN NICHOLAS TO THE RESCUE

Black's life changed one night in early 1987, when Hayden Nicholas showed up to replace another guitarist who had taken the proverbial powder. "Hayden and I met at a gig," Black recalled. At the time, he wasn't aware that he had found a song-writing partner, but he was very impressed with Nicholas' eight-track recorder. Since Black had been trying to make some demos of his original material but didn't have enough money to go into a real recording studio, Nicholas and his tape recorder were heaven-sent. "We worked out a deal to record some of my songs in his garage at a real reasonable rate."

It didn't take Nicholas long to figure out that he and his new friend were coming from a similar place musically, not failing to also notice that Black took his career very seriously indeed. "He had the voice and the looks, but more importantly, he had the ambition. He had the drive and the salesmanship people need," Nicholas says. "People envision this guy who grew up on horses, working cattle and listening to country music. But we were exposed to rock, blues and dance music. The Eagles were a big influence on me—that was as country as I would go at the time. So when me and Clint write, it's not going to be as traditional as Hank Williams. Probably nine out of ten conversations I have with fans, they say, 'I don't listen to country music, but I like y'all.' You see these guys in their pickup trucks and they'll have a Clint Black tape, and they also have Metallica." He added, "Clint didn't want the cookie-cutter approach. I feel we're doing traditional country, but we're not playing it the way they did twenty years ago."

The first tune the two worked on together was "Straight from the Factory," which would later become the lead-in track on *Killin' Time*. Then the pair set to work on "Nobody's Home." That tune, as well as "A Better Man," sprang from Clint's emotions over a romantic breakup. "A Better Man" addressed the real-life dilemma Black experienced when his girlfriend of seven years decided to move on—all the way to Belize in Central America. "I talked to my dad and said I was heartsick. He said, take advantage of that and write a good George Jones song." As for the woman in question, Black has never publicly revealed her identity—possibly out of respect for her privacy or his own. The passage of time has left him philosophical about the breakup. "She came back, but she left again." He sighed. "She may be anywhere. She's got a travelin' bone. But," and here his eyes crinkle up in that familiar grin, "I got a lot of good songs out of it!"

G.A. gave his boy some wise advice, which Black is now able to acknowledge, but at times—as with any parent and child—it got on Clint's nerves a little. "I was talking to my dad back in eighty-five about wanting to be a singer and wanting to write my own songs," he recalled. "He's a country music fanatic, lives and breathes it and always has, and is very partial to the traditional kind of country, and his remark to me was, 'You haven't done enough living yet. You haven't got enough time in the honky-tonks shooting pool, drinking beer, and getting into fights. You haven't lived enough to write good country songs,' " Clint remembered.

In his annoyance "I went home and wrote 'Nothing's News' in about twenty minutes. I ran back over and played it for him. Then I left him a copy of the lyrics, and he analyzed 'em and analyzed 'em this way and that. After about a month, he gave in and said that maybe, maybe I could write some songs." A proud G. A. said he's always believed in his son. "We all knew ten years ago that he *should* be a star, but there's so much luck involved, we didn't know if he ever would be. Well, now I know he's going to be a superstar. I just hope he can be happy with it. I think he will be. He's a pretty straight fella—doesn't smoke, hardly drinks. He brings bottled water with him over to the house. I don't think we ever have to worry about drugs or anything like that."

Black worked exclusively by himself before meeting and collaborating with Nicholas. "I wrote my first song when I was fifteen and got a lot of encouragement from my friends, so I started trying to do more of it. But I usually only did it when I was inspired by something that would happen. I never made a job of it until I was about twenty-four. Then I said, 'I'm just gonna lock myself in my apartment for three days and not do anything except write.' I would have two or three songs laid out on the table, and I'd work on one till I got stumped, then go to the other one and work on that. I literally did nothing but that for two or three days at a time."

Nowadays, their songwriting is a smooth-running collaboration. "The most common way it happens is Hayden or I will start with a musical idea and try to come up with a lyric," Black explained. "And we'll get away for a week, or two weeks if we're lucky, and work on five different ideas at a time. That's our magic number." He described using separate pieces of paper for each song lyric. "If we get stumped on one, we move on to the next one. We do it a lot like people who go into the office. . . . [it's] something like putting together a jigsaw puzzle."

He co-writes well with Nicholas, Black went on, because his partner is "not as particular about how the lyrics go, being that I'm the one singing them. He's more into the direction, the storyline and what it's saying, and the music. So he makes a lot of allowances in the lyrics for me. And I'll do the same thing with him a lot of times in the music." He goes on, "He's got theoretical training in music, and if he's saying we should go to this chord instead of that one, a lot of times I'll adapt my melodies to that direction."

In an early instance of the partners' ability to seize the moment, the title track of his debut album, *Killin' Time*, was created after Black made an idle comment. Although the lyrics are doleful, in the voice of a man who knows he is drinking himself to death and doesn't see much reason to stop, Black recalled, "We had big grins on our faces when we were writing it. The album had been in production for a few months, and I told Hayden, 'This killin' time is killin' me.' Right then, I knew we had a song idea. Though I was talking about the downtime in the music business, we took it in the direction of lost love."

As they worked on the music, Black realized that no matter how great the songs were or how well they were performed, they would be stuck on the club circuit forever...unless they could find somebody who believed in what they could achieve and could help make it happen. As he scuffled through the clubs in 1987, Black was offered a flat $250 fee to sell one of his songs outright to a local music publisher; he suspected that it had to be worth a lot more. Although he badly needed the money, he refused, reluctant to part with his work so cheaply. Black told this story to an independent Houston record promoter named Sammy Alfano and added that he thought he needed a manager. Two days later, Black was sitting in Bill Ham's office. It was the real beginning of his career, yet he would bitterly regret it in just a few short, sky-rocketing years.

CHAPTER TWO

KILLIN' TIME

When Clint Black sat down in Bill Ham's office that May afternoon in 1987, he knew that Ham managed Texas rock legend ZZ Top. The other thing he knew was that he wanted that kind of power behind him. "I was very, very headstrong in trying to find a record deal. This record promoter [Alfano] said, 'You know, if you could get with somebody like Bill Ham.' He said Bill Ham is probably the greatest deal maker in the business. When a record company sees him coming, they know he's got something good and that got me to thinking." Black went on, "My life changed when I met Bill Ham. . . . [He] got me an RCA contract. These people know how to set things up. I was just going around in circles until I found Ham."

Black recalled that Ham told him that he "was looking for a country act, and had looked at hundreds over the years." After listening to Black's homemade demo, Ham invited him to an office audition. "I remember him sitting there grinning, with the fellows who head his publishing company and his management, and they're all sitting around and Bill's going, 'Well, play me something *else* that you've written.' I played him every song I'd ever

27

written on the acoustic guitar, and he put on this big old grin and looked over at his folks, smiled, and said, 'Boy, that's really good country.' I didn't feel any pressure. I was a little excited, of course, knowing this could be the turning point for me." He remembered, "It was all very simple to me. I wasn't ever going to go to Nashville or Los Angeles or New York. My intention was to get something together here and find a manager. And when I met Bill and we worked out our deal for management, production, and publishing, that was it. After you get your management in order, you can just be an artist." Black's naiveté would eventually cost him dearly, but that was years down the line. And he wanted to break out of the club circuit, badly. "I knew I had to get out, or I was going to wear my throat out, because I sing pretty hard."

So it didn't take Black long to decide to sign on the dotted line. Asked if he could have gotten a contract sooner if he'd met Ham earlier in his career, Black concluded that his timing was, in fact, perfect. "I had gotten to the point where I could demonstrate my songwriting ability. I could demonstrate my singing ability, and if it had happened any earlier, I might not have been ready." And, lo, it came to pass: in just six months, he was signed to RCA Records, and work on his debut album began in earnest.

The buzz on the street started immediately: this kid was someone to watch. Long before the album came out, folks in Nashville had heard about this young, hungry Texan and were keeping an eye on him. And Black, not one to disappoint, burst out of the corral running. When *Killin' Time* was released in the summer of 1989, "A Better Man" raced up the *Billboard* country charts straight to number 1, the first debut single to do so since 1975. The album

With singing star K.T. Oslin (opposite page). Backstage at "Geraldo" with country sensation Alan Jackson (above).

sold almost a half-million copies in three months. In June, the *Boston Globe*'s Steve Morse marveled, "Clint Black has come out of nowhere. . . . [He] is a heart-on-sleeve singer in the vein of Merle Haggard and Randy Travis, with a pinch of Lefty Frizzell. . . . His voice, which sounds instantly timeless, has a world-weary wisdom that breathes dignity into the saddest of songs. . . . There's no contrived ego here; just a guy trying to make ends meet and find a woman who won't have him crying in his beer."

He got a bigger hand from an even more prestigious source. Veteran critic Jay Cocks wrote in the September 11, 1989, issue of *Time* magazine about Black's earliest appearances at family barbecues, adding: "The music is a lot more refined than his back-

Clint chats with Geraldo Rivera during his appearance on the popular television show in November, 1990.

XXXXXXXXXXX

"Entertainment Tonight"'s Leeza Gibbons accompanies Clint in New York City, January 1991.

yard material, and it doesn't come with ribs, but it's the freshest, pithiest country sound since Randy Travis. . . . Black's got a good ear and—judging from his songs—short patience for affectation of any kind. His lyrics bear down sharp but easy, perhaps because he came to country by a slightly different route (rock and roll.) . . . What (Garth) Brooks and Black share, along with a winning penchant for hit-making, is a gift for finding something fresh in the familiar, something timely in the predictable and shopworn. In uptown kinds of music, that quality is called soul. Down home, it's just known as country. Pure country."

In August, *Rolling Stone* weighed in with its own opinion, which was every bit as prestigious as *Time's*, especially for a younger, hipper, record-purchasing target audience. It was a coup for any artist to have a debut record reviewed in the magazine, but it must have been particularly sweet for Black, whose rock and pop heroes had been profiled and reviewed in those very pages. "In today's brave new Nashville," Holly Gleason wrote, "artists fall into neat categories: the docile crooners like Randy Travis and George Strait, who sing pretty and pretty much toe the line, and the hell-raisers like Steve Earle and John Anderson. But, lucky for us, twenty-seven-year-old Clint Black

31

doesn't fall into one of the neat categories. Neither choirboy nor hellion, he writes and sings about battered hearts, broken dreams, and tortured emotions with an unflinching directness. The best thing about *Killin' Time* is Black never sounds like he's trying too hard. Like Merle Haggard, Black understands striking veins of emotion is the real deal. . . . This is a lean, hard country record . . . and the backbeat is meant for dance floors. But that doesn't make it an album for hillbillies and rednecks only. Anyone who's ever known a dull ache that won't go away will find themselves in this music."

Black was on his way; he landed a spot opening for K. T. Oslin on her tour, and continued to win good reviews from jaded big-city reporters when the bill played New York's famed Carnegie Hall. "Nashville's young heartthrob stood center stage strumming his acoustic guitar while a five-piece band embroidered his hard-boiled melodies. . . . What has made Black instant competition for Randy Travis and George Strait, however, are his original songs. 'A Better Man' . . . already sounds like a classic with a telling twist," wrote John Milward in the October 7, 1989, New York *Newsday*. "That's the kind of country that works from the Grand Ole Opry clear to Carnegie Hall." Indeed, *Elle* magazine noted, "At Carnegie Hall, cowgirls could be seen standing on their seats in the second balcony and hollering their approval."

While he might have been understandably nervous about playing such a prestigious hall, Black wound up enjoying himself, saying later that the crowd was so appreciative, he felt as if he were back in "Austin on a Saturday night." He figured that even big city dwellers could understand where he was coming from and respond in kind, because, as he put it, "Rock 'n' roll talks about fast cars, fast women—which are beyond the reach of the average guy. Country lyrics talk about real life, the more common things, like all the alimony you pay." And, just like their kissin' cousins down in Texas, New Yorkers could relate to that.

When Black left Carnegie Hall, the applause still ringing happily in his ears, he was abruptly brought back to earth by a note tucked under the windshield wipers of his tour bus, parked directly outside. It read: "Yo, Clint, loved the show." It was accompanied by a ticket for illegal parking. Black discovered then that New York's finest could be just as hard-nosed as advertised.

Undeterred, he returned to New York the following month, when he participated in a more joyful Big Apple tradition: the

The years of practice paid off — Clint performs at one of the most prestigious music venues in the world, Carnegie Hall in New York City, October 5, 1989 (opposite page).

33

Macy's Thanksgiving Day parade. "I'm going to be wearing my thermal underwear," he said proudly, "and sitting on the big turkey float. That's going to be something. I don't think a person could be more exposed than that." The featured country artist in the parade, Black admitted that the whole thing "was hilarious to me." As it was for many other American families, watching the parade on television was a tradition in the Black household. "Nobody paid much attention to it, but it was always on." This year, he reckoned, his parents and brothers might be looking up from the turkey a bit more often.

Black was hitting his stride. He was even getting used to the demands of the press eating up much of his limited time to himself, and even enjoying the rigors of publicity, sometimes. "When

Backstage with super-star Randy Travis at the 1991 Country Music Awards.

they first sent me out on a radio tour to promote the record," he confided,"when I started talking to the press, I was nervous. It was the unknown. I didn't know how the people perceived me, how I perceived them, how everything fit together. But from the moment I got my feet wet, I liked it. I was calling my management saying, 'This is *great*. Let's do this some *more*.'" Black laughed with delight. "Everyone I've talked to cares about country music, and they've made me feel like I've done something good, like I'm welcome. I'm surprised, really, that things are going this well."

Black went on to open a few shows for Randy Travis, almost stealing the headliner's thunder out from under him. Black admires Travis and has acknowledged his debt to the first huge crossover country star of modern times: "Before Randy Travis and George Strait came on the scene," he said, "most people used to think traditional country music was just a bunch of old crooners singing torch songs." Reviewing Black's set during one of those knockout double bills, Long Island *Newsday* wrote: "Singing several selections from [his first] album, Black proved to be a diamond in the not-so-rough, handling his set with aplomb. . . . He and his backup band, on their first stop in the New York area, also seemed genuinely pleased—and surprised—at the warm reception from the audience, whose whoops and hollers—and a bouquet tossed on stage by a shy preteen in a party dress—brought some broad grins."

Black was having a good time onstage, delivering renditions of Fats Waller's "Ain't Misbehavin' " cheek by jowl with a cover of James Taylor's "Steamroller Blues." "It's exhaustingly exciting," he exulted to *USA Weekend* in October. "It just wears me out to be having so much fun." He was also trying to get used to having money. "It still feels really strange to gather up five hundred dollars and go into a Western-wear store and spend it. I remember thinking to myself, What's it going to be like when I can go in there and buy everything I like?" He soon found out, telling one interviewer that he preferred ostrich, python, or eel for his dress boots, while cottoning more to elephant, iguana, and shark for "kicking around." On the other end of his body, he explained, "I own lots of white hats, but I don't like them." His trademark black hat, he said, was probably due to the genetic influence of that violin-playing great-grandfather from Sicily: "Italians like black."

Black was shopping around in more ways than one, it seemed. "There's a number in my book," he sheepishly admitted to a

35

reporter, "that I don't have to look in my book to get . . . but we have an understanding that we can't have a commitment. Settling down is a luxury that I don't see me able to afford for quite some time. . . . You've got to want that hour in front of an audience to spend the other twenty-three doing what you've done to get to that town. I've got that obsession." So much so that he would only go home to check his mail and messages when he played Houston, preferring to sleep in a hotel in his own hometown. "You have to stay in the road mode," he explained. "Otherwise, it'll wreck you." He spoke from experience, having once tried to stay at his house during local dates. There wasn't enough time, he said, to slip back into his old routine, and he left feeling less relaxed than when he'd arrived. "It was weird."

His workaholism, however, was beginning to pay off. By the fall, Black had been nominated for three awards by the Country Music Association: best single, best song ("A Better Man"), and the Horizon Award for career advancement. Black was eager for the recognition. "I want it!" he said. "I'm after all those [awards] I can get. I'm a red-blooded American. I was brought up with Little League and all that. Those trophies really mean something to me." He went on, "I'm up for competing with anybody and anything. If you don't have that [attitude], there's nothing to the award. There's some tough competition this year, but that's what makes it exciting. If you get called up there, you know you've really accomplished something." He was called up when he won the Horizon, a coveted harbinger of later success. Beaming, he told reporters covering the awards, "Now I feel I'm stepping into the picture."

After Kenny Rogers announced Black as the Horizon winner, friends and family watching TV in Kelso's, a Houston club where Black used to perform, erupted in cheers. "You would have thought the Oilers had won the Super Bowl," said an eyewitness. "Hugs all around. . . . A few wiped away tears." In the middle of the club, Black's brothers Kevin and Brian embraced while surrounded by friends. Their parents were in Nashville with Clint, and brother Mark had a family matter that kept him from attending the booster rally. Brian exulted, "It was unbelievable." Kevin added, "There was no doubt in my mind. I just knew he would win." He added that he didn't plan to stop harassing his little brother anytime soon: "I suspect we'll pick on him even worse. He'll know he's got it coming when he comes home for Christmas."

Afterward, Black confessed that in the heat of the moment, he made a significant omission in his speech. "I had so many people I wanted to thank. When I heard my name called I said to myself, just relax, take your time, remember to thank everyone—then I forgot to thank mom and dad. Fortunately"—he grinned—"I was able to thank them later."

Black's star was rising ever higher. A panel of country music insiders were asked to predict who would sell the most records over the next seven years, the average length of a standard recording contract; Garth Brooks finished narrowly ahead of Black, by only two points. Said one panel member, "In many ways, we are talking one and one-A in terms of potential when we talk about Brooks and Black. To me, Clint is a little sexier, feistier—a little mischievous. . . . Who's going to sell the most? It depends who'll come up with the best material." Another panel member commented, "Don't underestimate the charisma and the looks. He's sexy—not in the self-conscious way of Dwight Yoakam—but in the style of Johnny Cash or Merle Haggard." And still another added, "He has the ability to sing in a bluesy, funky way, which gives him the potential to cross over into the pop field without losing his country touch or following."

Back in March, just as the first single, "A Better Man," was being released, Ham and then–RCA Nashville chief Joe Galante decided to leave nothing to chance and set up a promotional tour of every top country radio station in the nation, aimed at charming the DJs and program directors. *Killin' Time* had come out in May, which is when Black "officially" hit the road. The charm was beginning to wear off; Black was experiencing his first real bout of road weariness when he told one writer, "I tell you, pardner, this travelin' leaves you a little fuzzy sometimes. I don't know where I am or what day it is 'bout half the time anymore. Travelin' like I been doin', well, it's like havin' one of them *wild* honky-tonk weekends, you know? Yeah, boy, I can relate to them wild weekends." He started to laugh, then stopped. "Funny thing is, I just don't know whether my weekends come on a Monday or a Friday anymore." Still, he knew it was all part of the game. "Things been happenin' pretty quick for us. And I hope that it gets even more ridiculous. I tell you what, I'm havin' the time of my life."

All the hard work was paying off, though; Black was wowing them out on the concert trail. The Richmond, Virginia, *News-Leader* said, "Black's band backed him up with tight, seamless

At the Country Music Association Awards in Nashville, October 1989, after winning the Horizon Award for career advancement.

38

energy that made every song irresistibly danceable. . . . Clint Black has competition among the current crop of good-looking, good-sounding male singers in country music, but nobody puts on a show that makes you smile any bigger or feel any better than he does."

One person Black made feel better was a little girl named Missy Turner, who lived in Great Kills, New York, a long way from Texas. Turner, who was three and a half years old, suffered from severe breathing problems; her parents needed to raise money to bring her to London, where they hoped she would receive experimental drug treatments. Her mother, Theresa, met Black at the Country Music Awards and asked if he would help. "There was something about this man," Theresa told the *Staten Island Advance* on July 17, 1989, the day after Black played the benefit for her daughter. "He was so warm and sincere, I knew he was going to be the one to help Missy. We thought he'd just be another singer who'd come and say hello, Missy, and leave—but he did so much more. . . . He supported her from the minute he saw her." The girl's aunt, holding her at the benefit concert, said, "I think she feels the love that is in this room. She's radiant tonight." Black headlined the benefit, at $25 a ticket, and praised those in attendance prior to his performance: "It's extra special to know there are all those warm hearts in the audience." Mrs. Rutledge (Missy's aunt) felt she knew who had the warmest heart of all. "He came to us at a time when there was no hope, and he gave of himself."

Black attended his first Fan Fair and was overwhelmed by the response. "It's just what you pictured it to be," he said. "With the record company people ushering you around, it's everything I imagined it to be. Walking by crowds of people who are goin', 'Hey,' and all you can do is grin at 'em and smile. I know where those grins and waves come from now. Just when I think I've given my last smile and I'm exhausted, the crowd'll light me up. To quote myself from *The Wall Street Journal,* 'It'd give a dead man energy.' "

In case the fans didn't rev his engines enough, Black was now the proud possessor of a red '87 Porsche, courtesy of an offhand comment by his record producer, James Stroud. "I told Clint, 'Kid, you get me a gold record and you can have my Porsche.' I was able to hold off when he went gold, but when he went platinum [selling a million copies of *Killin' Time*], I pretty much had to give it up."

At this point in time, Black was beginning to feel the heat of his newly found sex-symbol status. The screams from the audience both puzzled and pleased him. "Somebody said, 'Do you have this problem everywhere you go?' I said, 'Is it a problem?' Oh, no. If I went anywhere I didn't get attention from 'em, I'd see that as a problem." "I'm very single," he announced to one writer, "and I've got an ego like anyone else. If what happens to George Strait happens to me, too, it'll be a great thing. You won't hear me complain." He mock-protested to another, "I hate it, I really do," but he was chuckling when he said it. "It's tough, I tell you. It's tough havin' to walk away from all those beautiful women every night. It's a lonely life. But I'm fightin' it." He got more than his share of propositions, but the weirdest of all, Black told *People* magazine, had to be the woman who approached him at an autograph session, plunked down her fingernail clipper in front of him, and demanded a few of his fingernails. "I don't know what she could have wanted them for, but I had just spent so much time gettin' them right, scrubbin' 'em and filin' 'em down, I just said, 'No, you can't have my fingernails,' " he said, shaking his head in bewilderment. Marriage proposals and requests for locks of his hair, he told the magazine, had become routine. He'd even received a batch of letters from a group of fourth-grade matchmakers, suggesting that he marry their teacher.

Some fans went a bit over the top, even by the looser standards of the lovelorn. A wire service story of December 6, 1990, reported that a thirty-eight-year old woman, Karen Herring, of Jackson, Mississippi, had seen fit to dress up in a French maid's outfit and submerge herself in a tub of steaming noodles for a half hour (along with a six-month-old piglet named Clint). She would prove to be the most determined entrant in a local country radio station contest, and won tickets to Black's show. Attempting to explain her temporary insanity, Herring told the press: "I'm a big Clint Black fan. I just wanted to go see him." That didn't cut much ice with her fifteen-year-old daughter, Mindy, who simply said, "She's crazy."

Black seemed to have that effect on women of all ages. "Sometimes I don't entirely understand it," he admitted, "because I've seen some crazy things, some girls who just can't control themselves. . . . One girl grabbed my pant leg and had a good hold on it. [I nearly] went out into a sea of twenty thousand people." During a somewhat smaller club date in Cape Girardeau,

Missouri, fifty-two-year old Stella Bailey confessed to *The Wall Street Journal* after observing Black's performance: "He's one of the best I ever heard. I've been drinking, but I think that even when I'm not drinking." The younger women in attendance just giggled and snuggled up for photos with the star.

That would have been better than a ticket to heaven for Brenda Reynolds and her two daughters, who drove more than ninety miles from her home in Lebanon, Tennessee, to Clarksville, just for the opportunity to watch Black shoot the video for "Put Yourself in My Shoes." "We've just gotten to see him through the door, but even that's been worth the drive," Reynolds told a reporter during her six-hour wait outside Owens' barber shop, where the video was being taped. "I'm close to him. That's enough." Radonna Owens, the shop owner's daughter, got to watch the action from inside. She, too, was taken with Black. "Clint is just a doll," she told a local newpaper. "He's been super nice."

But even though he now had a wider field than most men to choose from when it came to the opposite sex, the double-edged sword of fame brought unexpected difficulties. "I can get a date now," he admitted, "but, uh, well, it's hard to know who the person is and why she's interested in me. I could grab up somebody, I guess, and take them to Vegas or Colorado because there's a lot of pretty women. But I like good conversation, and it's hard to know if you're going to have any of that."

He told *Country America* magazine in September 1990 that he still hadn't found what he was looking for. "I'm a romantic at heart," Black confessed, "and I still love the idea of getting married. But . . . I'm going to give myself at least four or five years. You would imagine I would at least be able to grab a date here and there." He grinned and shook his head. It was 2 A.M. in Las Vegas, and he was just getting off work. "But, oddly enough, it's just not like that. After a show, by the time I get around to going somewhere, all the opportunities are gone. I don't have a girlfriend, and I am looking."

He wouldn't have to look long. By the end of the year, he would meet Lisa Hartman backstage at one of his shows, and his lonely nights would be ancient history.

CHAPTER THREE

LISA HARTMAN

Lisa Hartman left her native Texas to conquer Hollywood back in 1975, while Clint Black was still considering whether he should become an astronaut. The ambitious blonde had several things going for her, including sensual good looks, a lion's mane of blond hair, and startling sky-blue eyes, along with a knowing glance that hinted at a smoldering sexuality. She also had a strong-willed stage mother, Jonni, who aided and abetted Lisa's own fierce determination to be a star.

Hartman had originally moved to Los Angeles to make her mark as a singer. "Yeah, I wanted to be the next Olivia [Newton-John]," she told a reporter. "I wanted to be huge. I wanted to cut the LP and get the Grammy. I never thought about other things." She made her first album, *Letterock*, in 1982; it was reviewed in *People* magazine less than kindly. "Hartman's run-of-the-mill voice is helped little by lackluster songs and lame instrumental arrangements. If only she sounded like she looks." Undaunted, Hartman told an interviewer in 1984, "I'd like to be the female equivalent of Rick Springfield," a pop singer who had also starred on a soap opera and had a minor hit with "Jessie's Girl" before fading from view.

43

Lisa Hartman with actress Michelle Lee at the dinner following the "Night of 100 Stars II" at Radio City Music Hall in New York City, February 1985.
XXXXXXXXXXXX

At that time, she was at the halfway point of her four-year stint on the prime-time TV soap opera, *Knot's Landing*, playing first the role of singer Ciji Dunne (1982–'83), and then, with impeccable soap logic, Cathy Geary (1983–'86). *Knot's Landing* would prove to be her longest lasting success.

Her acting career had begun with a brief experience in children's theater back home. Soon after moving to Los Angeles,

Rehearsing in Los Angeles for an October 1979 performance at Harrah's in Reno, Nevada.

A 1984 publicity photo at the time of Lisa's second run on "Knot's Landing."

Lisa strikes a sexy pose in January 1984 as the news broke that her "KL" character, Cathy Geary, would be featured in the cliffhanger season finale.

47

48

Hartman landed a role as a witch in the short-lived TV series, *Tabitha*, a spin-off of the popular *Bewitched*. *Tabitha* ran for only thirteen episodes, but Hartman tried to put a cheery spin on its demise. "After all, it was a hit in its time-slot during summer reruns," she told the *Los Angeles Times* in 1987. "I believe things happen the way they do for a reason, whether it be in your professional or personal life."

Hartman said she "had a wonderful, normal childhood. I played ball, but I also played the Supremes and acted like I was Diana Ross." The practice in front of the bedroom mirror paid off: by 1981, she had developed a nightclub act and made two ABC-TV television specials, *Hot Stuff with Lisa Hartman*, and *You're Never Too Old*. She had a feisty streak that made for good copy, like the interview she gave that summer to a reporter for the syndicated wire service, United Press International. "No matter what the statistics say, women motorists deserve their reputation as lousy drivers. . . . Most of them are afraid of snapping a fingernail or having their hair blow when they open a window. They really don't concentrate on what they're doing." Hartman continued. "Part of the problem is conditioning. It's considered unfeminine to take charge behind the wheel. It's not ladylike to drive aggressively, like men."

The reason Hartman was dishing lady drivers was her pride in the fact that she had recently placed third in the destruction derby at Houston's Auto Thrill Show, held in the same Astrodome her future husband would headline a decade later. The purpose of a destruction derby, for the unenlightened, is for twenty or so competitors to crash into one another as often and with as much speed as possible, damaging the vehicle—and perhaps the driver—in the process. It's an elimination contest; the car that remains running at the end of the carnage is the winner. Obviously, it's not a pastime for the faint of heart, but that was never Hartman's problem.

"My ultimate dream is to star in a race car movie," Hartman commented to the same reporter. "I've been driving since I was eleven years old, down in Texas. My dad used to let me sit on his lap and steer the family car when I was eight. . . . I'm mad about automobiles. . . . I'm fearless when it comes to driving."

She seemed to be fearless in her career as well. She dropped out of what seemed a secure gig on *Knot's Landing* in February 1986, releasing a statement to the effect that she had signed a

I n character
with handsome
series co-star
*Alec Baldwin,
April 1985
(opposite page).*

49

singing contract with Atlantic Records and wanted to pursue that end of her career. Not one to box herself in, she cagily told reporters that she hoped the writers wouldn't kill off her character, so she could return later if she wanted to. The executives at the network saw it differently: offended at Hartman's defection, they arranged for her character to be bumped off.

Hartman's departure turned out to be premature, in light of the reviews and sales of her 1988 album, *'Til My Heart Stops*. It was savaged by *People* magazine, whose critic found the record "banal . . . dull. . . . There's nothing wrong with this album . . . that a few terrific songs wouldn't fix in a snap." Music lovers seemed to agree; the record went nowhere in a hurry.

Hartman, at loose ends, attempted to keep a high profile in Hollywood, showing up at show-business functions semiclad in sparkly, navel-baring gowns that impressed the paparazzi, but not, alas, the casting agents. Despite her best efforts, her career never reached the heights she had hoped for when she first arrived in Tinseltown. Instead of the Oscars, Emmys, or Grammys she had once coveted, Hartman received dubious awards such as "Most Expressive Eyes" in an annual poll of Hollywood makeup artists. The president of the organization declared that Hartman's orbs were "both sensitive and alluring." Still focusing on her physical attributes rather than her acting talent, the Guild of Professional Hairstylists named Hartman one of the "best-tressed" women in the country, along with Joan Rivers, Cybill Shepherd and Jamie Lee Curtis. It was the type of recognition that wasn't of much use when it was time to pay the rent; and the lack of professional acclaim must have wounded Hartman, who has defined herself as a perfectionist. "Everything I do, I hope is better than my last," she told a reporter. "It's the way I look at it all. That's why I'm hard on myself."

She made a forgettable foray into feature films with a swimsuit epic entitled, *Where The Boys Are '84*. Unfortunately, more distinguished offers were not forthcoming. As big-screen stardom continued to elude her, Hartman—much like the actresses Victoria Principal, Valerie Bertinelli, and Jane Seymour—concentrated on television work. She managed to carve out a niche in soap-style movies and miniseries, such as the 1987 *Roses Are For The Rich*, in which she co-starred with Bruce Dern; *Where The Ladies Go*, and *Valley of the Dolls*. By the time 1989 had rolled around, Hartman was starring in *The Sex Tapes*, which she described as "a murder-mystery-blackmail-power-money-sex [TV] movie." Part of her research for the role took her to the seamy side of town. "I went with friends to S&M bars to see what the life style was like—I couldn't believe how much was out there. It was a real shock."

It didn't seem to faze Jonni Hartman, who was more than just a stage mother. Jonni was a publicist whose main client was her daughter. When she wasn't guiding Lisa's career, she could revert to more traditional concerns, telling her in front of an interviewer in 1987, "I know why you're not married." Sensing what was coming, Lisa groaned, "Oh, no, mother." Undeterred, Jonni delivered the clincher: "You can't cook!" (Hartman's reaction was not reported, perhaps because it was unprintable.)

As it turned out, her cooking skills, or lack thereof, wouldn't pose a problem for Clint Black.

CHAPTER FOUR

WALK A MILE IN MY BOOTS

While Lisa Hartman was deciding which route to take in her acting and singing careers, Clint Black was forging full speed ahead with his second album. The conventional wisdom in the record business holds that a follow-up to a strong debut can be a pitfall if not handled correctly. The so-called "sophomore slump" is explained by the dictum, "You have twenty-five years to make your first record, and only six months to make the second." But, in a good example of his ability to think ahead, Black came prepared, writing much of what would become *Put Yourself in My Shoes* while working on *Killin' Time*.

He told one reporter while he was out on the road, "The songs that were written for the second album were written at the same time that several of the ones were for the first album, so it was all pretty much chosen from the same catalog." It was a good thing he had the foresight to keep some backup, since he didn't much care for writing while touring. "I don't try to mix 'em. If something comes spurting out, I'll let it, but I don't try real hard to write while I'm out here. I think I'd just confuse myself into believing I couldn't write 'em anymore. I have actually written a few since last year

53

Clint and his band bring their high energy music to New York's Radio City Music Hall, August 9, 1991.

when we started touring, though". He admitted, "But we're gonna take some time for that. I believe that when you write, you go off and don't do anything else.

"I've learned it can be a craft, that when I want to write a song about killin' myself and drinkin' myself blind, I can do it without having to be in that situation and without having to be inspired to do it. I can pretty much decide I'm going to write a song like that and do it. At least, without mixing it with recording and touring, I think I can. We'll have to wait and see," Black concluded.

55

He did, however, confess to a tiny touch of the jitters, "You want to try and take it one at a time, but you still can't help but think of the first album. I'll have to say I could feel some pressure, not like anyone was leaning on me, but just as an artist to go in to do something better than the first one." He added, "I've given it some thought. As long as the songs can stand up and compare in quality in my mind—I trust my judgment there."

THE RECORD'S OUT AND THE REVIEWS COME IN

By the fall of 1990, *Put Yourself in My Shoes* had arrived, to rather mixed reviews. Alanna Nash, a freelance critic and author concentrating on country music, brought a gender sensitivity to her review in the February 1991, issue of *Stereo Review*: "[This] is an album that does everything the first one did, but shows Black to be a writer of even greater poise and agility. . . . He again maps out the domestic and emotional terrain of the traditional working-class male, but he redraws the borders for both the stereotypical country protagonist and the music he appreciates. . . In decades past, a virile country singer wouldn't be caught dead hinting that he might put himself in a woman's shoes—someone might think he wears her dresses, too. . . . These are modern men—men who are looking for real relationships rather than instant gratification. . . . In other words, Black's protagonists are men who want to grow up, not postpone adult responsibilities as long as possible. . . . His second album moves him on down the road to proving himself a talent worthy of playing with the best in the big time."

New York *Newsday* was more guarded in its take on the album. "Clint Black is both the present and the future of country music. . . . You have to give Black credit. His debut album of last year. . . . was an enormous hit: double platinum and Number One on the country charts for seven months. There are worse places to be standing than in those kind of shoes. But when a singer is expected to match that kind of success with his or her second album—and they always are—it's almost a no-win proposition. To Black's credit again, however, he seems to have put all the natural inhibitions aside and turned out a record which, had it been his first, would be as impressive as *Killin' Time*."

"Anyone thinking Black could be a flash in the pan best think again," declared the *Chicago Tribune*. "The young singer-song-

A happy fan realizes that meeting your favorite singer is good, but having him autograph your shirt is even better. At Nashville's Fan Fair in June, 1992.

writer masterfully and emotionally sings a new batch of songs as skillfully written as those on his debut. . . . Black's intelligence should keep him from crumbling as country music's ever more impressive waves of new artists wash over the scene." *Billboard* magazine said, "It is as musically solid as its predecessor. . . . It is also distinguished by splashes of lyrical poetry and myth. Black, who wrote or co-wrote all the selections, sings with engaging conviction and candor."

The *Washington Post*'s reviewer was a bit chillier, opining that *Shoes* was "not nearly as consistent as *Killin' Time*," but added, "The album does hold some surprises . . . the songwriting . . . is more ambitious this time around . . . his voice holds up well here."' And the *Los Angeles Times* was the frostiest of all; the reviewer felt that Black was striving "too hard to be all things to all fans. He's a honky-tonk swinger here, a restless balladeer there, a working stiff, a lover—never just Clint Black. He's capable of keen observations and neat turns of phrases, but often settles for such things as 'No man is an island, but I'm still all alone'. . . . More often (than not) the album hinges on the music (expertly executed, but there's not a lick that's not recycled) and Black's voice (he's good, but hardly the pure singer that, say, Randy Travis is). And that leaves pretty much just the grin and the brim."

ON THE ROAD AGAIN

The mixed reviews didn't seem to have much of an adverse effect on Black, though he could have been keeping up a good front. "It's hard to subscribe to the trades [music business magazines] out here on the bus. If I'm not Number One, then no one lets me know where I am, so I usually don't know unless I'm Number One. If my album didn't get there, I'd have to look around and see who was doing so well that it didn't." And he kept up his punishing pace on the road, telling one writer, "I wouldn't be in the place I am today if I didn't go flat out. It's been crazy, but necessary." He staved off boredom on the bus by listening to his favorite music: "Chet Atkins, Steely Dan, Buck Owens, Little Feat, Jimmy Buffett, [James] Taylor, Dan Fogelberg. I've got all kinds of

Performing the Grammy-nominated "Hold On Partner" with Roy Rogers in Nashville, October 1991.

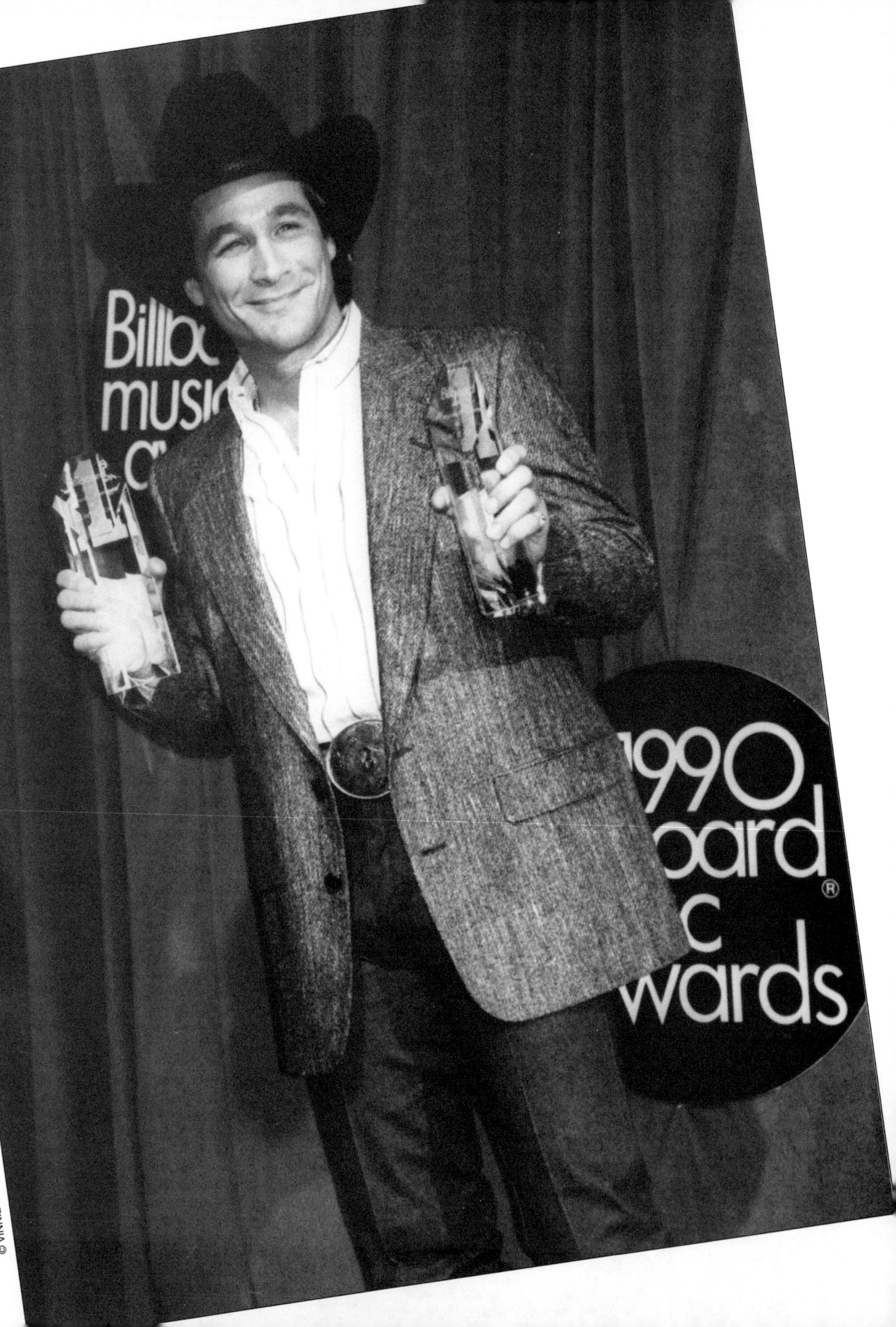
1990

stuff in there. . . . I've got about 160 CDs that I carry around. You gotta have it."

Still, the road was taking its toll. Black had just survived the 1991 Fan Fair in Nashville, where *Billboard* found that he and Garth Brooks were the favorite artists of the twenty-four thousand fans in attendance. That kind of popularity can exact a price. Black sounded as if he was tiring of the routine a bit when he admitted "Usually, I sleep on the way in and just wake up in the front of the hotel. But the road's getting a little long."

He kept his sanity, he said, by being aware of the pitfalls that had claimed other singers in the past. "I learned a lot from Hank and Elvis," Black said. "It was hard on them, because they had no examples to live by. But I work out in a gym and eat healthy. I don't look at this as a party. That's where they made their mistake." The discipline and strength that were part of the fiber of Black's character were serving him well. But he would need those qualities, and more, in the wake of a shocking crime that destroyed his manager's life and rocked his own.

A DEATH IN THE FAMILY

Cecile Ham, the wife of Black's manager Bill Ham, had been missing for six weeks when her body was found near San Antonio, Texas, on August 10, 1991. A twenty-two-year-old parolee named Spencer Corey Goodman was charged with murder after he admitted kidnapping and killing Cecile, forty-eight. On the afternoon of July 2, Goodman said, he had spotted Mrs. Ham in the parking lot of a Walgreen's drugstore in Houston. Actually, it was her flashy red Cadillac that caught his eye, according to Houston detective Billy Belk. "He told us that his primary motive was to steal the car, and he didn't know why he killed her," Belk said. Goodman knocked Mrs. Ham unconscious, driving ten miles before he decided to kill her by breaking her neck.

Afterward, Goodman drove to San Antonio and dumped Mrs. Ham's body in a nearby field. He was found in Colorado August 7, after police traced his use of Mrs. Ham's credit cards. He was still driving the red Cadillac. Black, upon hearing the dreadful news, canceled interviews and immediately made plans to fly to Waxahachie, Texas, to be at his manager's side for the funeral. Goodman, who had past convictions for burglary, car theft, and

Clint proudly displays the Billboard Music Awards he received for his number one single ("A Better Man") and number one album (Killin' Time) (opposite page).

61

parole violations, was convicted of the murder after giving three separate confessions to the police. He was sentenced to death after an emotional two weeks in court, which Bill Ham attended almost every day. Goodman's death sentence was automatically appealed, and he still sits on death row in Texas.

Ironically, less than a month later, a concert review of Black's September appearance at the Seattle Center Coliseum reported, "After watching his show, it's hard to believe the smiling, likable country singer has ever felt sad in his life. Joy radiated from the stage as the young star and his fine six-piece band romped through most of the cuts from their two albums." It also must have helped Black's state of mind somewhat to receive the Songwriter of the Year award from ASCAP, the performing rights society, that same month.

Black and Nicholas took a short break from the road to vacation in Hawaii, where they worked on material for the next album. It was a luxurious locale, but by now Black could well afford it; by the end of the year, he would be named one of the top ten touring acts of 1991 by *Amusement Business* magazine, with ticket sales amounting to $12.6 million. And Black didn't appear to know the meaning of the word "rest": besides working with his steady partner, he had already managed to fit in a couple of collaborations with two of his earliest heroes.

Having often been compared to Roy Rogers for his squinty-eyed grin, it was almost inevitable that Black would consider a joint appearance with the veteran cowboy star when the opportunit arose. It looked like a father-and-son reunion when Rogers joined Black for a charming duet, "Hold on Partner," which wound up being nominated for a 1991 Grammy for Best Country Male Vocal Collaboration. Black said of their work together, "It was really cool. He's a great guy, full of anecdotes. I get excited every time I think about him. It was just really special being in the video with him, just a really special time." Rogers joked that Black's headgear put him in mind of all the villains he'd dispatched in the movies, telling reporters, "When I saw him coming at me with that big black hat, I said to him, I thought I killed all you guys."

Merle Haggard, another man with whom Black had been compared many a time, had "been on tour with me all year except for twenty dates in August," Black told an interviewer. "He and I have finished one song, and we're working on another. It's really great to be working with him. He's country blues at its finest. In fact, he's got all kinds of styles that people haven't heard—jazz, blues, or blues-jazz as they'd say in *Spinal Tap* — he's got all kinds of things up his sleeve."

And, Black added, he had learned something else from the veteran: "Watch out for your money. If they take one million dollars, it'll take three million dollars to get it back."

Black could hardly know it at the time, but Haggard's advice would prove sadly prophetic.

CHAPTER FIVE

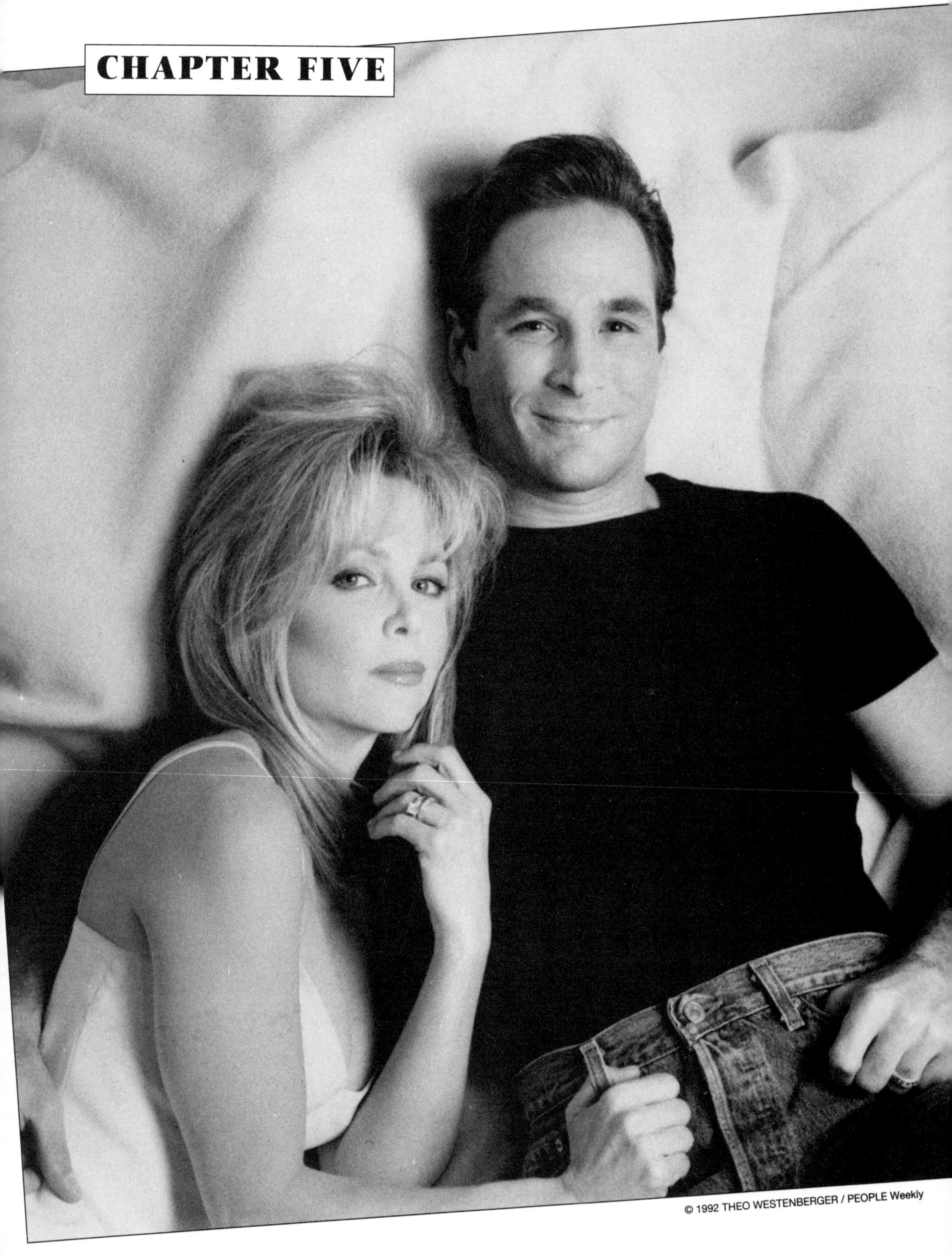

A WEDDING . . .

By the end of one of the most trying years of his life, Clint Black had come to one realization: Lisa Hartman was the best thing in it.

They had met backstage in their hometown of Houston, on New Year's Eve 1990. "I was knocked out by the show," Hartman recalls. "Then I went backstage and was knocked out again." Black had been equally smitten. "There were about two hundred people backstage that night, but with those beautiful blue eyes, she stood out in the crowd." It wasn't as unlikely an attraction as it might have seemed on the surface. Black said, "The truth is, Lisa lives in cowboy boots and jeans and is from Houston and is more down to earth than I am. . . . Anybody who knows me could never figure that we were a strange combination."

Black later gave a more detailed description of the meeting that changed his life. "So we met backstage, said hello, talked about the show, and then said, see ya. That was it. I was in a real bad place physically and mentally. I had really been stressed out from the road and my throat was in real bad shape and I just felt

65

Both Clint and Lisa have hectic schedules, so they never miss an opportunity to spend time together, whether frolicking with their dog or enjoying a quiet moment at home.

awful. I wasn't looking forward to the reception and I just went out there and she stood out and it was, I don't know, I hate to sound corny, my spirits, you know," he stumbled, momentarily at a loss for words. "It was great. She had beautiful blue eyes. It was uplifting at a time when I was ready to go crawl in a hole for a month. Over the next month and a half, a lot of people were coming up to me saying, 'Oh, I heard you met Lisa Hartman, you ought to call her. You two would really hit it off.'

"Meanwhile"—Black grinned—"she's got the same thing; people saying to her, you guys would be perfect for each other. We had all these matchmakers around us. I came out to L.A. for the American Country Music Awards in the spring and called her up and invited her out to dinner. We hit it off real well, saw a lot of each other over the next week or however long I was out here. It was great, but it wasn't what it is today."

And today? "She makes me better. She makes me more than I am. At the same time, she gives me room to be less than I am when I'm not. She's my best friend." He admitted that, "It wasn't love at first sight. It took us a while to realize that we weren't going to be able to live without each other, and once we knew, though, it was strong and definite, and we knew we had to stand up in front of the world and tell everybody that we had made the commitment." He told another reporter, "The reason I was able to marry Lisa after knowing her such a short time is 'cause I knew she understood the commitment. It's *much* easier to just walk away and try again." This time, neither would take the easy way out.

After a whirlwind six-month courtship, conducted mostly in Los Angeles and Nashville (with a few stolen days in Toronto and Hawaii), he proposed to her in Salt Lake City in September, and she accepted. "We just grew real close real quickly," Black confessed. Hartman mused, "You know what I think it was? We had the same morals—we're both considerate and fair. I'd seen him in interviews, and I knew he was a solid man. I felt like I could trust him. I think that's why we kept on seeing each other, even though it wasn't love at first sight."

Black, twenty-nine at the time, and Hartman, who admits to thirty-five but—like many actresses—is said to have "forgotten" a few years, were wed on his 180-acre farm outside Houston on October 20, 1991. Tellingly, Bill Ham was not among the guests.

A photo opportunity for Clint and Lisa backstage at the 1992 American Music Awards.

"We wanted to keep it very simple," Black said. "Just say what we wanted to say to our families and make our promises to each other." Hartman concurred. "Both of us are very blessed that we have terrific families. There's a lot of love there and a lot of support. The wedding was our way of sharing our love with them." As if to underscore her point, Hartman had her sister, Terri, as her matron of honor.

Under an arch of flowers on the porch of the farmhouse, the couple exchanged diamond-inlaid wedding bands and recited the vows that Black had written expressly for the ceremony. Hartman sighed, "It was so beautiful. I don't think I'll ever forget the moment. . . . I got a little nervous because there was so much going on. Then I came around the corner and saw his face, and he was all I could think about." Black, in keeping with tradition, did not see his bride before the ceremony: he changed into his tux on his tour bus.

Up until then, she hadn't planned on ever getting married, and Black certainly hadn't expected it to happen to him so soon. As recently as July, he had been telling people, "I'm home about three days a month and I'm real selfish with my time. . . . I go into a relationship knowing how it is and I lay my cards on the table. At least if the relationships don't last, there's not the heartbreak." "We both had the same fears about marriage," Hartman said, "but when you meet the right person, you know." Black echoed her sentiments: "How do you know? You just know. You just feel like you couldn't live without her. . . . It's funny. I've watched so many of my friends get married, and their nerves are on edge, but I didn't have any of that. I was just so happy, so at peace—and so relieved that I was gonna have this woman with me for the rest of my life."

When both partners are in show business, though, the prosaic question of how to live in the same place at the same time becomes problematic. "We both like it up here in Nashville," Black confided to a reporter a few months before their first anniversary. "It's really pretty. We've got a great place up on the lake, and my dog can swim, and we've got a canoe and fishin' poles. On the other hand, L. A.'s got its advantages. Neither of us are big party goers, or big night lifers, but there's a lot of things you can find here [Los Angeles] that you can't find in a smaller town. And she's got a job [the now-canceled TV series, *2000 Malibu Road*] that's pretty much gonna anchor her to one town, so what are you gonna do?"

And with two high-powered careers under one roof, the question of whether to have children takes on added dimensions. "That's a full-time job," Black said, "and neither one of us is prepared to give our time to it right now. We're pretty selfish with each other whenever we have time to ourselves. But you never know. Two years from now, we're liable to be jumpin' up and down tryin' to have a baby. The one thing I've learned is what I believe today certainly will change."

CHAPTER SIX

...AND A D·I·V·O·R·C·E

One thing that was about to change was Black's relationship with his manager, Bill Ham. In February 1992, Black announced his intention to split with the manager who had helped bring him to prominence. Ham, who had reportedly invested a million dollars of his own money in Black, wasn't about to take it lying down.

In March, both men filed lawsuits, each accusing the other of breach of contract. Black released a prepared statement to the press, saying, "It was shocking to recently discover that the financial aspects of my business relationship with Mr. Ham were grossly one-sided and served to enhance Mr. Ham's personal interest at my expense financially and professionally. I have only just begun to understand some of the things that have been going on and being done in my name. Throughout the history of our relationship, Mr. Ham has repeatedly failed to provide me in a timely fashion, if at all, with copies of contracts and financial accountings I have requested.

73

Bill Ham (far right) with ZZ Top drummer Frank Beard (second from left) and two guests backstage during the 1990-91 Recycler tour.

xxxxxxxxxxxxx

"Mr. Ham has apparently expressed his concern over the quality of advice I am receiving. I am pleased to say that after terminating my relationship with Mr. Ham, I no longer suffer from that problem."

Bill Ham promptly fired back his own salvo, describing Black's charges as "a thinly disguised, self-serving attempt to escalate a business dispute and degrade it into a personal smear campaign. . . . As a result of my carefully planned and executed efforts, and the services of the team of professionals I put together to help guide Clint Black's career, he has skyrocketed in four years from being an unknown, starving musician to living the life of a superstar celebrity and enjoying his status as a multimillionaire. Clint knows it did not just 'happen.' "

Ham was not alone in feeling that Black was being manipulated by his new bride and his publicist mother-in-law. Lisa was

already being referred to as "the Robin Givens of Nashville" by people along Music Row. "When I read Jonni Hartman's scurrilous press release," Ham stated with no little heat, "I cannot believe in my heart that Clint had anything to do with it, as I consider the attack unworthy of him. Now that Clint no longer wants us to manage him, I regret that lawyers have become involved, but that is inevitable when so much money is at stake."

In May, it got even more acrimonious. Black filed a more specific cross complaint, charging Ham with fraud and breach of contract. Ham held all the copyrights and publishing rights to Black's songs, and,

*W*ith Carlene Carter during the announcement ceremony for the 1991 CMA Awards nominations at Opryland Park.

along with merchandising, publishing is where the money is in the music business. Black also charged Ham with refusing to obtain a million-dollar-plus Miller Beer tour sponsorship, unless he paid Ham 30 percent of the proceeds. The going rate, as stated in their management contract, was 20 percent. According to the court papers, Black went along because he "fear[ed] that he would not be able to make any type of deal with Miller Brewing Company unless he agreed to the proposition." Having secured Black's "reluctant" agreement to the seven-figure deal, the suit continued, "defendant Bill Ham receiv[ed] an additional commission of several hundred thousand dollars."

In addition to seeking damages in excess of two million dollars Black wanted Ham to return more than four million dollars he felt Ham wrongfully received. Moreover, he wanted Ham to forfeit the publishing rights to mechanical and public performance royalties which he had sewn up in his own publishing company, Hamstein Music, for Black's first eight albums. And to top it all off, Sammy Alfano, the Houston promoter who had introduced Ham

75

and Black, was cut in for a share of Black's publishing rights. How common is it for a manager to retain all publishing rights or to split them with a third party, other than an artist or songwriter? "That's highly unusual," concedes one industry observer.

Don Engel, the L. A. music attorney Black hired to represent him against Ham, went even further. "These days, managers advise their clients to keep control of their own publishing, and [Ham] was the one who advised Clint to do these things. We're talking about millions of dollars here." He later added that Black "has learned facts that make him very indignant about what Ham did to him."

Ham hired a Los Angeles legal eagle of his own, Joseph Schleimer, who told the press, "Mr. Ham is getting exactly the commission [on the sponsorship deal] that Clint Black agreed to pay him, not a penny more, not a penny less. . . . If you had spent ten years playing honky-tonks and getting rejected by record companies, and a guy came along who said he can make you forty to eighty million dollars from your music career, would you pay twenty percent for that? . . . Clint Black was just a guy with a guitar. Mr. Ham invested one million dollars of his own money in Clint Black's career at a time when nobody else would do so. For that commitment, Mr. Black should show a little gratitude and honor his contracts."

It was getting more complicated and uglier by the minute. When had it all begun to sour? In early 1990, Black was praising his manager to *Billboard*: "With the master plan between Joe Galante [RCA Records executive] and Bill Ham, I've got a foundation that should last me the rest of my life. I've got the wildest dreams—and with everything that happens, they just get wilder and bigger." But by October 1991, as noted previously, Ham was conspicuously absent at his star client's wedding. Industry gossips whispered that Ham's insistence on a pre-nuptial contract had alienated Black and infuriated Hartman. In the end, these insiders believed, the couple did sign a prenup, which was said to have been drawn up by Hartman's lawyer.

In January 1992, Black hired Jonni Hartman as his "personal assistant." A month later, Black went public with his lawsuit against Ham. The break, and the strong personalities involved, made the situation the talk of the music and show business communities in three states. In Nashville, many in the country music industry perceived Lisa and Jonni as pushy carpetbaggers, fearing that the two harpies would take their golden boy and turn his head, take him "Hollywood." In Houston, an observer noted, "In country, you're supposed to marry your high school sweetheart. If Clint were a rock star, the marriage wouldn't be seen to be so deleterious." In Hollywood, there was the usual cynical talk, much of it centered on speculation that the marriage could be a boon to both of Hartman's career goals, if she could only persuade her handsome husband to act or record a duet with her.

Black defended his new family. "These stories about my mother-in-law managing me and my wife and her control of my life [are] utter nonsense," he told a reporter. "I can't comment on [reports that both Hartman ladies were behind his split with Ham]. But I can tell you that what happened was inevitable, and it would have happened if I had never met another woman, or person, on the face of the earth."

With Patty Loveless during the Music City News/TNN Awards held at the Grand Ole Opry in Nashville, June 1992.

XXXXXXXXXXXXX

. . . AND BABY MAKES ONE TOO MANY

The brouhaha with Ham was not the sum total of Black's legal entanglements. His own record label, RCA, filed suit against him, asking the court to confirm the rights of BMG Music, the parent company, to Black's exclusive services. They dropped the suit when he renegotiated his contract in April— without Bill Ham's participation. But the next legal battle was even more emotionally upsetting: a woman from Phoenix, Arizona, appeared on the tabloid TV show, *A Current Affair,* in March 1992, charging that Black was the father of her two-year-old daughter, and that he had abandoned both her and the child. Renee Bain sounded bitter, saying that she was "so tired of everybody thinking that Clint is this wonderful person."

Bain said that she met Black after one of his performances in a Phoenix nightclub. One thing, as it will, led to another, and the child, whose pictures she held up on the air, had been the result. "I told him I was pregnant . . . he was shocked. He didn't know what to do. He was scared. And I understood. He was trying to get a career going. His first record was getting ready to be released. I want her to know who her daddy is," Bain said plaintively, "especially if he's a celebrity."

According to Bain, a blood test had established with "99 percent certainty" that Black was the father. She added that he had agreed to pay $800 a month child support, but had been keeping his distance from her and the child since his marriage. Black's lawyer, who indicated that his client would "continue to meet his legal obligations," had allegedly sent a letter to Bain saying that Black wanted to sever all ties to the child.

Jonni Hartman, who has the reputation of being a tigress when it comes to protecting her daughter, told *USA Today* on March 12 that she had never heard of the child, and refused comment from her clients. Hartman and Black were "vacationing." When questioned about the matter later, Black would only say, "I can't comment on that; I won't comment on that." He had to have been torn up inside over the entire mess. (Jonni Hartman has resigned from Black's account, and he has since acquired new management.)

No wonder he would be calling his next album *The Hard Way*.

STARTING OVER

After all the disappointments of their first year together, Black and Hartman still had each other, and for them, it was more than enough. "We're inseparable. The tabloids were kind to us at first, and we thought we were pretty lucky. Then I heard somewhere that we got into a fight in a parking lot and stuff like that, you know. It couldn't be farther from the truth," Black maintains. In fact, almost a year after their marriage, the couple posed for an article that appeared in the November 1992 issue of *McCall's*, entitled "What Makes a Man Feel at Home," in which Black admits that his favorite room is the bedroom. The story is accompanied by a full-page color photo of Lisa in bed, wearing shades and reading—of all things—*The Anatomical Products Catalog*, while Black and his big black pooch are curled up on the floor at her feet. He is strumming a guitar and gazing wistfully out at the reader. "The bedroom is my favorite place," Black said, "because I have a great marriage. It's where my wife and I spend most of our time. We've got a big-screen TV in front of the bed and a stereo system—CD and DAT player and cassette player—all the things I need to do my work.

81

*C*lint greets
Emmylou
Harris and
legendary country
music producer
Owen Bradley at
the BMI Awards in
Nashville, October
1992.

XXXXXXXXXXXXX

82

"The photo on our nightstand is our wedding picture. . . . The photographer caught the moment when we were both over-whelmed with joy, and that picture just takes us back. We're still honeymooners, you see." Sigh.

He burbled to an interviewer,"1989 was a great year and 1990 was better and 1991 topped that. And here I am in 1992 with a great marriage and great career. It makes someone stop and wonder, can it be this good?" He said that he'd only received one negative letter from a fan regarding his marriage. "She was mad at me because she said I said I wasn't going to get married and I was lying. Like I knew. She thought I was concealing this long-time relationship. It [meeting and marrying Hartman] literally

The almost whimsical domestic scene, as it appeared in the November 1992 issue of McCall's.

C lint greets a young fan at a record store autographing session during his 1989 tour for Killin' Time (opposite page).

happened to me in the course of about six months."

Black felt fortunate to have had such a strong ally in his corner during the trying time he'd just been through with his ex-manager. Asked what Hartman offered him, Black responded, "Support. She's my best friend and partner in life, and she takes care of me more than I ever thought anybody would, or could. She's made me much, much better than I was and better than I ever thought I could be in every way. She has made me a better person."

Even the stars seemed to smile on their pairing; an astrologer told *USA Today* in January 1992 that the chances of marital success for Black and Hartman, who were among the star-crossed couples she had been asked to analyze, were good. "While he can be somewhat detached at times," the astrologer declared, "this relationship is full of fun and delight."

Fun was the last thing on Black's mind when he entered the studio to begin work on his third album. "I initially went into the studio back in November (of 1991) and preproduced the album, which is what I had always wanted to do," he told an interviewer. "I had always wanted to spend time working on it and looking at it before doing it for real. So we cut in November and a little bit of December, then resumed in February and March."

Despite all the bad feelings that had surrounded the Ham lawsuit, Black was determined that this record be a strong one. "See the most important thing is, once that album is out there, it remains that way for the rest of my life. That's my piece of art, and it'll either stand the test of time or not. That's what matters most." He went on, "I'm happier than I've ever been. In the face of the adversities, I still maintain that nothing matters but the music, and that's why I'm here. You know, if I weren't getting paid, I'd probably still be fighting to do it."

He hesitated when reporters asked about the messy breakup with Ham, mostly in consideration of their ongoing litigation, but the frustration was very close to the surface when he spoke. "I would love to talk about it. I can't *tell* you how much I would love to talk about it. And I can't," Black told *Us* magazine in November 1992. "Part of me would like to just settle this thing and go on. [But] the much stronger feeling I have is to go to court."

"It's not a very happy situation, but it doesn't affect me," Black admitted; "Professionally, I don't think you can go through a transition like that without stumbling a bit. I'm a very driven person,

84

and I'm very, very ambitious when it comes to my music and my career, and it didn't take me long to look at things and figure out where I wanted to go and what I wanted to do. Personally, it's easy for me to leave that stuff to the lawyers." He continued, "I've got so much to do out here, so much to think about, it's not hard for me to leave it to the lawyers, and that's what you're supposed to do in a case like this." Black told an interviewer, "I can compartmentalize things really well to the point that they don't plague me; it's not a monkey on my back."

He gave a more revealing glimpse into his personality when he said, "I have felt the full range of emotions—remorse, anger, relief, and happiness. But no matter what pain and suffering come from doing the right thing, you've got to be able to recognize what you have to do and be thankful for recognizing it. I'm a very realistic person. My principles are very strong. When things become clear to me, I will do what's right at all cost." He added, "I have within myself a large capability for looking to the bright side. In my life, it's not hard. I have a lot of bright sides. It's just a matter of, if you've got to chop down a tree, it ain't going to fall over [by itself], so get started. And when you get a blister on your hand," he continued, "don't complain. The tree's got to come down, and if a blister's got to come from it, then you're going to have a blister."

Despite his matter-of-fact attitude, it appeared that Black continued to harbor darker feelings toward Ham and worked them out the only way he knew how: in his music. When *The Hard Way* was released, several critics discerned a "bitterness and anger unprecedented in Black's earlier work," ascribing the vented rage in songs like "Something to Cry About" to the singer's battles with his ex-manager. Hayden Nicholas offered a deeper insight on the rift. "It hurt him," Nicholas said quietly. "Clint looked at Bill like a father and was very defensive of him. It's the old expression—you can't really hate somebody unless you've loved them. Before, Clint was naive in some ways. And I hate seeing him lose that, 'cause I think that's a lot of his charm - his genuineness, always believing the best about somebody. He's a little more distrustful now," Nicholas concluded, "a little more businesslike."

Black was pleased with the album's progress, noting that he finally had the creative control he'd been seeking on this record. He commented that, on his second album, he had been running all over the country, laying down a vocal track here, overdubbing there. "It was crazy, it was not me," Black explained. "I hate to put the project down, because there were so many people involved, but it was not the greatest effort. I was able on this new album to be in there, not only physically but mentally, and not wanting to leave the studio because I needed some rest. . . . I was able to influence my record more so this time than any other time."

SONGWRITING FOR FUN AND PROFIT

Black has been unique among country stars for writing most of his own material with Nicholas. While several critics feel that he would benefit from more outside input, Black has been stubborn on the issue. It could be a matter of both ego and finance. The ability to write one's own material contributes to career longevity, and Black has made it clear that he intends to stick around for a while. Songwriting is also extremely lucrative, and publishing royalties can be a gold mine, even if other singers never record a cover version of the material. For example, every time an early Lennon-McCartney song (which includes all the Beatles' biggest hits) is played or performed by another artist, Michael Jackson makes money. Jackson had cannily purchased Northern Songs, which published those hits, when Paul McCartney and Lennon's heir, Yoko Ono, could not come to terms on the price. McCartney himself is no pauper, holding the rights to all of his solo material as well as Buddy Holly's catalog. It's an investment considerably more secure than speculation in the stock market. Utilities rise and fall, but "That'll Be the Day" goes on forever.

Black's falling out with Ham had much to do with control of his own music publishing. If he didn't write his own songs, Black said, "I'd be sitting with my producer listening to a catalog [of songs] that Reba [McEntire] has listened to, George Strait has listened to, Vince Gill, Ricky Van Shelton—everybody's listened to it already, you know they have. So what are you going to find that they've passed on? The number of great songs sitting around Nashville is very small, and you've got a lot of people looking. If we need an up-tempo song for the album, it's much easier for us to take a day, or maybe two or three days, and write it than it is to sit and listen to a catalog of a thousand songs and hope we find it."

E very perfor-
mance needs
to be perfect,
so rehearsals are
an integral part of
daily life for Clint
and his band, as
seen here during
the 1992 Hard Way
tour.

88

89

Black, according to Rick Mitchell's comprehensive story in *Request* magazine, had been receiving pressure from his record label to record outside material. He told Mitchell in no uncertain terms that he didn't see the need. "When I got to the third album, they started getting concerned. They wanted me to be open to outside material, and I am. I said, 'Guys, whenever I doubt myself, if I ever feel I don't have ten songs that could be radio singles, then I'll listen.' And I have listened, but nobody has handed me anything I felt deserved to be on my album more than one of my own songs." He added that if he ever did record a cover, he would rather revive an older song, like Steve Miller's "Dance, Dance, Dance," or the Marshall Tucker Band's "Bob Away My Blues." It's also possible that a James Taylor tune could turn up someday: Black has been known to perform "Don't Let Me Be Lonely Tonight" at sound checks before his show.

"The Hard Way," the title track, was written when Black "was watching . . . somebody . . . longing for someone that they'd left or something like that, and I thought about my own situation, and although it doesn't work out, there's still a part of you that wants the good things from that." He went on, "So I just went real deep into those feelings and said, okay, never mind all the negative stuff, take it from the standpoint I'm not able to live without this person and I put myself in that place. I came up with this real lonely feeling, you know, that I'm finding out the hard way.

"I took it from that standpoint and tried to feel as lonely and as longing as I could in order to produce the song . . . It didn't seem like much at the time. It seemed like a nice little ballad. I even thought, well, you know, this is something that will probably end up on an album five or six albums down the road, whenever I'm searching for material and I'm not so far ahead of myself. Hayden really thought a lot more of it at the time than I did." Now, Black admitted, "I think that'll be the one I'll be most proud of, out of the three albums."

Black was preparing to get back out on the road to support his record, and the impending tour led him to muse on the deeper meanings of his celebrity. "I know who I am . . . I have to like myself for who I am, not for what I've done. I'm proud of my work, but no matter how many people love my work, I have to be a good guy every day, no matter what I'm doing . . . I have to go on my own credit as a person, not as a person who has sold five million records. So, regardless of the awards and the accolades, the crowds at the show and the people waiting backstage to meet me, that doesn't make me any more than I am." In the next breath, Black added a startling comment: "The only guy that can make me think more of myself is God. If God thought the world of me, I would have to really say, 'Okay, maybe I'm a great guy.'"

CHAPTER EIGHT

© 1992 P.F. BENT

DOING THINGS THE HARD WAY

The *Hard Way* was released in mid-July 1992, fully nineteen months after *Put Yourself in My Shoes*. In the interval, Garth Brooks had ruled the charts; and he was ready to release not one, but *two* new albums in early autumn. The pressure was on. Black had to deliver, and deliver big.

It wasn't as simple as dueling egos; there were huge amounts of money at stake. As Rick Mitchell explained in his editorial, "Why Clint Black's Accountant Is More Important Than His Bass Player," in *Request* in August 1992, "Becoming a star ought to be about having the best voice or the most talent overall, but that's not always, or even usually, the case . . . Hoping to match Brooks' megasuccess . . . the record company wanted Black to record outside material to maximize his odds of selling as many records as Brooks. . . . RCA wanted Black to mimic Brooks' work methods, also. . . . RCA is a subsidiary of BMG, one of the two least successful of the six major record companies that control the music industry. To BMG, Black isn't simply a country star but a cash cow for a corporation engaged in a financial shootout for world domination."

Warming up during the Music City softball game at the beginning of Fan Fair week in Nashville, June 1992.

It was a long way from the O. K. Corral.

Black knew how high the stakes had become. "The main reason I got into [the music business] was to entertain people. I've been doing it since I was fifteen, and somehow it turns into the General Motors Corporation." He said that if the record didn't do well, "I won't point the finger at me and say, 'You made a mistake in recording the album you wanted to make.' I'll look around and see if I did something else. Was it the delay? Was it the press about me and my record company and my former manager? But no matter what, this is the record I wanted to make. I like the album, although I won't listen to it anymore. I've already listened to it a thousand times."

94

*T*HE CRITICS HAVE THEIR SAY

Now it was the pundits' turn to listen. Mitchell, writing in Black's hometown paper, the *Houston Chronicle*, was one of the first to weigh in on the record. "*The Hard Way* might be the silver lining to Clint Black's dark cloud. Just as the best songs on *Killin' Time*, Black's landmark debut album, were prompted by his painful breakup with a longtime girlfriend, so has Black's messy legal divorce from manager Bill Ham provided him with inspiration . . . [the album] is a reflection on lost illusions . . . of the ten tunes on the CD . . . no more than two or three take an optimistic view. . . . Although Ham's name is never mentioned and the lyrics

95

Rockabilly
legend Carl
Perkins jams
with Clint during
the celebration for
the release of
Perkins' new album
at the Hard Rock
Cafe in New York
City, January 1992.
✗✗✗✗✗✗✗✗✗✗✗✗✗

are directed at former lovers rather than ex-managers, it's difficult not to read between the lines . . . most of the album is about pain and loss rather than love and happiness, and that's the source of its power."

Alanna Nash, writing in *Entertainment Weekly*, thought that "If 'Killin' Time,' Black's startling 1989 debut, took an upbeat, though fatalistic, look at blue-collar love, and *Put Yourself* captured the tension of a young man scrambling to find himself, *The Hard Way* is about delusion, lost innocence, and hard-won wisdom. Only a smattering of the songs reflect a halfway hopeful attitude." Nash wasn't alone in singling out the tracks "Something to Cry About" and "Burn One Down" as sounding as if they were aimed directly at Ham. She concluded, "The record succeeds as Black's premier experiment in musical cross-pollination . . . Black skillfully and subtly insinuates enough traces of pop melody, aggressive rhythms, and soaring, soulful instrumental solos . . . to carry his work to a broader audience. Whether these listeners can handle Black's downer of a catharsis, however, arriving like a doubled-up fist to the jaw, will probably depend on their view of romance in the confrontational 1990's." The record, in the style of the magazine, was graded B minus.

Black's history of mixed reviews continued as he set off on tour. Jon Bream wrote in the October 31, 1992, edition of the *Minneapolis Star Tribune*, "The first hour of last night's performance suggested that Black's songs make better radio music than concert fare. Not even huge hits as 'Better Man' and 'Nobody's Home' could galvanize the crowd." However, Bream added, "Without his [trademark] hat, the black-clad singer cut a dark, dashing figure. He seemed as friendly as the guy next door and likably modest and appreciative for a superstar with a Hollywood wife, Lisa Hartman, who was sitting at the sound-mixing console at the back of the arena."

The *Los Angeles Times'* Mike Boehm wrote of Black's show nearly a month earlier, "Black's presentation showed pure class . . . As a singer, [he)] was controlled and firm, letting good material speak for itself without trying to show off or overdramatize. His solid talent showed in classic, catch-in-the-throat maneuvers during high, plaintive ballad passages and in some bluesy vocal slides. . . . The concert was helped along by an intelligent structure and by the adventurous bent (by Nashville standards, anyway) that the Black-Nicholas partnership sometimes takes in its songwriting."

Boehm added, "Black appears to be one of the last, best hopes mainstream country music has to develop a star songwriter-performer with a distinctive personal vision . . . It will be interesting to see whether Black can follow his most interesting, unorthodox inclinations—and if so, whether he will pay for it by being run out of Nashville."

2000 MALIBU ROAD

Meanwhile, Hartman was trying to get back on track with her career. She made a pilot for a show called *2000 Malibu Road*, in which she would portray Jade, a newly retired prostitute whose sudden dip in income forces her to rent out part of her posh beachfront home. The premise makes one wonder where Hollywood gets its ideas for TV series, although one of the creative partners on *Malibu* defended it by saying, "Most of the shows are about people whose lives are more boring than mine, and I don't see where that's entertaining." Hartman's tenants were to include Jennifer 'Flashdance' Beals and Drew Barrymore, *E.T.*'s childhood friend, a veteran of rehab before she was old enough to vote.

Hartman told reporters that she thought the show had a lot to do with the way many people lived their lives today, with support groups of friends and roommates taking the place of the scattered nuclear family. "I don't think there are a lot of traditional families," she said. "We talk about 'traditional values,' but what is that? This is a very sexy show, and I think these are interesting women, and it is real life...whether one wants to admit it or not." She told another reporter, "I've seen Oprah and Donahue .. . . with four to five twisted people on their panel five days a week. There are no Cleavers out there." But one critic scoffed in the *Vancouver Sun*: "This is not really about family values. It's about tits and ass, and you know, this is really exploitive stuff."

Hartman was confident that she could balance working on the show, if it were to take off as a series, with her personal life, even though her husband would be touring for the better part of the year. "We all have days off occasionally, and when mine is a Friday or Monday, I take that long weekend and spend it with him." Black, for his part, couldn't wait for the weekends. He said

99

Clint with singers Stacy Earl and Bruce Hornsby at the RCA party held at Tatou in New York City following the 1992 Grammy Awards ceremony (above). With Suzy Boggus, and Too Slim of Riders in the Sky during the taping of the Country Music Hall of Fame Anniversary show at the Grand Ole Opry, May 1992 (right).

100

101

that he could see the difference in his life now that he was married. "Being out here on the road away from my wife makes me realize there's something a lot lonelier about being lonely alone." But he did give her credit for stamina, claiming, "She doesn't travel nearly as much as I do, but she travels a whole lot better than I do." Insiders, though, said that Hartman never became truly comfortable traveling on the bus with Black; she was doing it out of a desire to please him.

When she came to Black's concerts, Hartman would often sit near the foot of the stage, smiling up at her husband and attracting a barrage of flashes from fans. Afterward, the couple would retreat to the tour bus, which was equipped with luxury appliances: stove, microwave, trash compactor, and full-size refrigerator. All things considered, the Blacks' life on wheels was remarkably like any stationary couple, according to Lisa. "He finishes [the show], and we come in here, and the bus pulls out. We read, we watch videos, and we have our own kitchen."

Despite Jonni's dire prophecy, Lisa had landed her man without having to imitate Julia Child; now she was making up for lost time. Black, in a bit of macho braggadocio, boasted, "Since she's been married to me, she's domesticated and she likes to cook." Hartman's specialties, according to Rob Tannenbaum (in *Us* Magazine), included nachos with low-cal chips, fat-free salsa, and sour cream. In addition, she whipped up pasta with fat-free sauce for her hard-working fella. She even played the gracious hostess, offering to make dinner for Tannenbaum: "Would you like something to eat? It's no problem." Despite the rumors that she wasn't thrilled about flying cross-country after toiling in front of the cameras only to spend her nights speeding down interstates and her days waiting through soundchecks until Black went onstage, to the reporter she seemed happy, relaxed, enjoying the best of both worlds: a handsome, devoted husband and a reviving career.

In late August, *2000 Malibu Road* was the Number One show in the ratings, and Hartman was over the moon. "Look at my face," she exulted. "I'm embarrassed and I'm thrilled. . . . It's so exciting!" Sadly, Hartman's employment was due to be short-lived. The critics, who with few exceptions had never been particularly generous to her efforts, loathed the show. *Road* was an easy target, since it was produced by Aaron Spelling, the man behind *Beverly Hills 90210* and *Melrose Place*, not to mention *Dynasty* and *The Love Boat*. Spelling had become a very wealthy man by having the common touch. Critics, naturally, despised the same shows that millions of people seemed to enjoy each week. Although Spelling thought *Road* was "just beautiful," one reporter seemed to express the general attitude of his colleagues after they were shown the pilot episode during the press tour: "Let me just get a recap of what we did see. We saw...a lineup of breasts, we saw lots of lingerie, a woman in lingerie being beaten up. . . . Other than bachelor parties, who is this supposed to entertain?"

The *Los Angeles Times* opined that the show was "pretty darned dumb," but its reviewer threw a crumb to Hartman and Beals for their "capable work." The *Washington Times* damned the show with faint praise when the review admitted that it "was not as awful as expected." That was a kind assessment compared to the review in *USA Today*, which called the show "an oil spill of rubbish [featuring] rank cliché and blank acting," and concluded that it was "toxic waste."

2000 Malibu Road was canceled in September 1992.

CHAPTER NINE

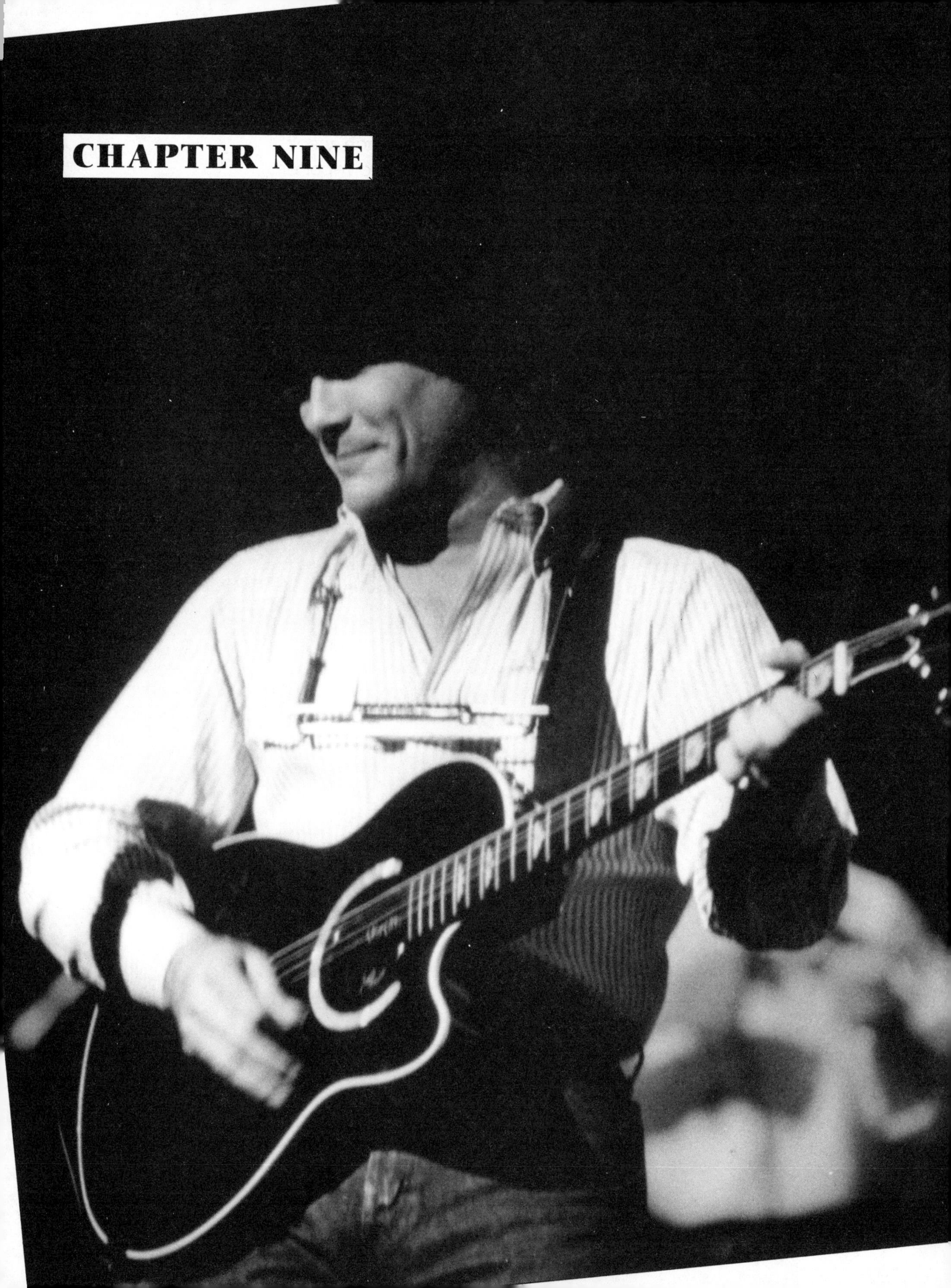

BACK
TO THE
FUTURE

After all his trials and tribulations, the question remains; where does Clint Black go from here?

The Hard Way tour has had uneven success: despite the quarter-million-dollar stage set and the grueling pace, Black is battling it out with other big artists (including Brooks) for limited concert dollars. While at least ten of Black's shows between December 1991 and October 1992 were sellouts, a minimum of another six were only half sold. The album, as of this writing (November 1992) is sliding down the charts, at the fringe of the Top 20, while two singles ("Burn One Down" and "We Tell Ourselves," the first two released off the record) are doing fairly well. Garth Brooks, meanwhile, is Number One—with "The Chase"—and Number Three, with his Christmas album, *Beyond the Season.*

Several insiders on the country scene were asked what they thought the future might hold for Clint Black. The following critics consented to speak on the record, while others would only comment for background.

105

A quiet moment with Lisa during a rehearsal break (below). Performing before a record sellout crowd at the live-stock Show and Rodeo in Houston's famed Astrodome, February 1990 (right).

Almost everyone agreed that Black's insistence on writing his own material exclusively with Hayden Nicholas has hurt him. Alanna Nash has followed Black's career from the beginning, reviewing his albums in magazines such as *Stereo Review* and *Entertainment Weekly*. An observant critic, Nash believes that "Clint just lost it on this last album. I guess the Bill Ham thing just turned his world upside down." She added, "Clint strikes me as someone who wants complete control, and he has a lot of confidence, which is sometimes misplaced. Unless he can come up with a very strong album, a very commercial album . . . he's in a psychological rut. He needs to get sparked. He should do what Randy Travis did, sitting down (and writing) with Alan Jackson. . . He's derivative, especially of Merle Haggard . . . and yet he [can] do something like 'Put Yourself in My Shoes' and manage to turn a fairly routine situation into a pretty pithy three-minute nugget of emotion."

Nash also feels that Black's marriage to Lisa Hartman may be a factor in alienating some of his fans: "It puts a stigma on his career. He's not supposed to marry a television actress . . . it makes him look somewhat superficial. It adds to a perception of [being] more interested in a Hollywood career than a long-term

dedication to his [country singing] career. There's a perception and prejudice on the part of the fans and it has nothing to do with logic. There's a he's-not one-of-us-anymore mentality."

Ed Morris, the country editor of *Billboard*, takes a different tack. "It seems to me that [since the break with Bill Ham] he's more at home with himself. He seems to be more sure of himself and have more enthusiasm. I would agree [with other critics] that some of his songs are weaker. . . . There was a period there when everybody thought he was getting a little too big for his britches. When he was with Ham, they [the media] sort of covered him like a rock star. He was criticized for allowing this. . . . From what I can tell, it was just the manner of management. I guess artists are terribly insecure people." Morris has a unique vantage point in that his daughter, a publicist for RCA in Nashville, works with Black. After Morris perused the court papers, his opinion of Black softened. "At first, I sort of followed the crowd and thought he sounded like an ungrateful little bastard, but the more I look and read about it. . . ." These days, Morris is more sympathetic to the singer, adding that if he were in Black's shoes, he might have felt the same way. "Not to have quick access to your manager, when you're on a roller coaster. . . ."

Even Morris, with his insider's perspective, can't quite pinpoint the moment when things began to change between Black and his manager. "After Mrs. Ham was killed, at that point, Clint seemed to be very sorry for Ham and would even cite Mrs. Ham in some of his concerts. . . . It's hard to know if this [the dispute with Ham] was a long time coming on. It seemed like there wasn't a rising enmity between the two, at least not from my perspective." Morris summed up, "I think there's still a good future for Clint. In a nutshell, I think he has the talent, the looks, and apparently the happiness to still have a good career ahead of him. It would take something more catastrophic than a dip in public opinion to throw him off the charts. . . . Obviously, he's never gonna be the big news again."

Rick Mitchell, who arrived at the *Houston Chronicle* in 1988, just in time to catch Black's last club appearances before he hit the big time, has perhaps the closest relationship with Black. As the music critic at Black's hometown newspaper, Mitchell has reviewed each Black album and interviewed the man many times. Mitchell chose his words carefully. "A guy who's sold five million copies of his first two albums really shouldn't have anything to prove. But the fact is, he does. While he was off the scene, the competition among young country artists increased to, I think, an unprecedented level. In 1989, when *Killin' Time* came out, you had Randy Travis and George Strait and Ricky Van Shelton. There was no Garth Brooks, no Alan Jackson, no Travis Tritt, no Billy Ray Cyrus, plus a lot of other people. I think that the legal problems he's had, and the publicity surrounding them, hasn't helped, but really, the main problem is, between the release of his second and third albums, a lot of people filled that void. Now he's going to have to re-establish himself. *The Hard Way* is a good album . . . not as good as *Killin' Time*, better than *Put Yourself in My Shoes*. As long as he continues to put out good albums, he'll remain a viable artist. Let's not feel too sorry for him." Mitchell added dryly, "*The Hard Way* has already gone platinum. Whether he can ever completely regain the momentum that he had with *Killin' Time* remains to be seen. I personally hope that he can."

Back when his first album came out, Black surmised that such a turnabout in his fortunes might come someday. "I've given it some thought," he said then. "As long as the songs can stand up and compare in quality in my mind—I trust my judgment there. If the popularity wanes a bit, I'll have to deal with it. The whole aim is just to try and settle in to where I can do this comfortably for the rest of my life."

And no one, not even the most reckless gambler, would lay odds against Clint Black's being able to do just that.

With co-presenter Roy Rogers at the 34th annual Grammy Awards, held at New York City's Radio Music Hall, February 25, 1992.

© VINNIE ZUFFANTE / STAR FILE

109

DISCOGRAPHY

(All compositions Clint Black/Hayden Nicholas unless otherwise noted)

Release Date
March 1989

Title
"A Better Man" (single)

Highest *Billboard*
Country Chart Position : 1
May 1989

Release Date
May 1989

Title
Killin' Time

Highest *Billboard*
Country Chart Position : 1
September 1989

"Straight from the Factory"
"A Better Man"
"Nobody's Home" (Black)
"Walkin' Away" (with Dick Gay)
"You're Gonna Leave Me Again"
"I'll Be Gone"
"Nothing's News" (Black)
"Winding Down" (Black)
"Killin' Time"
"Live and Learn" (Black)

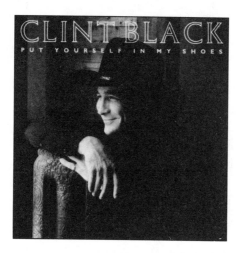

Release Date
November 1990

Title
Put Yourself in My Shoes

**Highest *Billboard*
Country Chart Position : 4**
December 1990

"Put Yourself in My Shoes "
     (with Shake Russell)
"The Gulf of Mexico"
"One More Payment"
     (with Shake Russell)
"Where Are You Now"
"The Old Man"
"This Nightlife"
"Loving Blind" (Black)
"Muddy Water"
"A Heart Like Mine"
"The Goodnight-Loving"

Release Date
October 1991

Title
"Hold on Partner"
 (duet with Roy Rogers on
Rogers' LP *Tribute*)

**Highest *Billboard*
Country Chart Position : 17**
December 1991

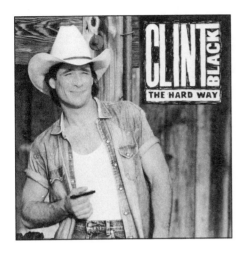

Release Date
July 1992

Title
The Hard Way

**Highest *Billboard*
Country Chart Position : 2**
August 1992

"We Tell Ourselves"
"The Hard Way"
"Something to Cry About"
"Buying Time"
"When My Ship Comes In"
"A Woman Has Her Way"
    (Black with Jerry Williams
    and David Bellamy)
"There Never Was a Train"
"The Good Old Days"
"Burn One Down" (with Frankie Miller)
"Wake Up Yesterday"

Clint Black International Fan Club

P.O. Box 299386

Houston, Texas 77299

April 25, 1990;
Clint proudly
displays his
Academy of
Country Music
award for Best
Single of the Year,
"A Better Man."

117